教育部大学英语教学改革示范点项目
教育部高等学校特色专业建设点（英语专业）项目
北京市支持中央在京高校共建项目"基于中西文化教育的大学英语教学改革"
北京高等学校"青年英才计划"项目（编号 YETP0783）
北京林业大学教改项目

总主编　史宝辉　訾缨

中国古代社会与文化英文教程

（第二版）

主　编　訾　缨　朱红梅
副主编　李　芝　罗凌志
编　者　（按所编单元顺序排列）
　　　　南宫梅芳　朱红梅　魏　文　李　岩　卢　辉
　　　　陶嘉玮　靳丽莹　欧阳宏亮　龚　锐　郭　陶

北京大学出版社
PEKING UNIVERSITY PRESS

图书在版编目(CIP)数据

中国古代社会与文化英文教程/訾缨，朱红梅主编.—2版.—北京：北京大学出版社，2015.8
（高等学校本科英语教改新教材）

ISBN 978-7-301-25446-2

Ⅰ.①中… Ⅱ.①訾…②朱… Ⅲ.①英语 – 高等学校 – 教材②中华文化 – 概况 Ⅳ.①H31

中国版本图书馆CIP数据核字（2015）第023301号

书　　名	中国古代社会与文化英文教程（第二版）
著作责任者	訾　缨　朱红梅　主编
责任编辑	李　颖
标准书号	ISBN 978-7-301-25446-2
出版发行	北京大学出版社
地　　址	北京市海淀区成府路205号　100871
网　　址	http://www.pup.cn　新浪微博：@北京大学出版社
电子信箱	zbing@pup.pku.edu.cn
电　　话	邮购部 62752015　发行部 62750672　编辑部 62754382
印　刷　者	三河市博文印刷有限公司
经　销　者	新华书店
	787毫米×1092毫米　16开本　11.5印张　360千字
	2013年8月第1版
	2015年8月第2版　2022年12月第4次印刷
定　　价	32.00元

未经许可，不得以任何方式复制或抄袭本书之部分或全部内容。
版权所有，侵权必究
举报电话：010-62752024　电子信箱：fd@pup.pku.edu.cn
图书如有印装质量问题，请与出版部联系，电话：010-62756370

第二版前言

由北京市教学名师史宝辉教授担纲总主编的《高等学校本科英语教改新教材》"英语话中华"系列之《中国古代社会与文化英文教程》和《中国当代社会与文化英文教程》是一套以英语为媒介传播和弘扬中华文化的高等院校文化素质类通识课系列教材,旨在通过对中国古代和当代社会历史文化等方面的介绍以及相关英语表达方式的训练,提高学生"向世界说明中国"的能力,在跨文化交际中能够熟练运用所学中国文化知识,以规范、流畅的英文表达方式对外宣传介绍中华民族悠久的历史文化传统,全方位、多角度展现今日中国之风采,让世界充分了解中国,增强中华文化的国际影响力。

本册为《中国古代社会与文化英文教程(第二版)》,全书共 10 个单元,建议授课学时为 30 学时左右,一学期完成;每单元分为两部分,Section A 和 Section B。通过听说读写等多种训练方式教授学生了解和介绍中华文化。Section A 包括两篇短文,通过阅读和写作训练方式使学生掌握如何介绍古代中国社会与文化的方方面面。Section B 包括一篇情景对话和一篇演讲或解说词,以听说训练的方式提高学生的英语口头表达能力和跨文化交际能力。

本教材的创新之处在于:

- 教材的编写和出版紧扣新时代主旋律,体现了党的十八大以来强调加强文化软实力建设和"让中国文化走出去"的精神;
- 契合教育部《完善中华优秀传统文化教育指导纲要》的主旨思想,以培养学生的人文素质和文化素质为己任,是新一轮大学英语教学改革的未来方向,得到了教育部大学英语教学改革办公室及大学英语教学指导委员会的一致认可,在新版《大学英语教学指南》中融入了这一教改理念。
- 教材通过以内容为依托,使学生在语言输出实践中不仅了解西方语言与文化,同时学会如何使用流畅、得体的英语将中国社会、政治、经济、教育、文化领域的话题进行话语构建和表达,从而实现语言与文化两个层面的输出。
- 该教材融知识性和趣味性于一体,图文并茂地提供了一种展现中国社会历史文化风貌的视觉方式,凸显重要主题,课程内容生动、直观,符合新一代大学生的认知心理。教材语篇长度、难度适中,生词采用文中注释的方式,文化背景知识注释采用脚注方式,方便学习和查找。每篇文章后均有长难句注释。
- 第 2 版对练习部分做了较大的修改,形式更加多样化,以提高学生跨文化交际能力为宗旨,以提高"写"和"说"的能力为突破口。练习的设计原则分为三个层次:第一个层次注重语言和内容的基础理解,第二个层次关注学生的思辨能力发展,第三个层次侧重语言输出能力的培养。特别增加了汉译英和段落匹配等练习形式,以期对学生通过大学英语四、六级考试有所帮助。

- 与教材配套的课堂版教学电子课件，制作精美，信息量大，使用便捷，有助于教师的备课和授课工作。在使用过程中，效果良好，受到了任课教师和学生的欢迎。
- 本教材读者群广泛，适用性强。主要读者对象为大专院校非英语专业本科生和研究生，也可供英语专业本科生和在华的各国留学生使用。

鉴于中国传统文化的英译历史悠久，版本繁多，本书所选文献所涉及的中国地名、人名、历史名词等译名呈现多种译法，有早期的威妥玛译法，亦有当代的汉语拼音译法，是中国典籍英译多样性的体现，并未强求一致。请任课教师在授课时结合中国典籍翻译历史，予以说明。

本教材是北京林业大学外语学院参与教育部大学英语教学改革示范点项目、教育部高等学校特色专业建设点（英语专业）项目、北京市与在京高校共建项目"基于中西文化教育的大学英语教学改革"项目、北京高等学校"青年英才计划"和北京林业大学校级重点教改项目"基于文化素养教育的大学英语教学改革"项目教师合作研发的产物，特此感谢上述机构对本项目研发的资助。

编　者
2015 年 8 月

《中国古代社会与文化英文教程》（第二版）

教 师 联 系 表

教材名称						
姓名：	性别：		职务：		职称：	
E-mail：		联系电话：		邮政编码：		
供职学校：			所在院系：			（章）
学校地址：						
教学科目与年级：			班级人数：			
通信地址：						

（教材名称行内容：《中国古代社会与文化英文教程》（第二版））

填写完毕后，请将此表邮寄给我们，我们将为您免费寄送本教材配套资料，谢谢！

北京市海淀区成府路 205 号
北京大学出版社外语编辑部　李颖　　　　邮 购 部 电 话：010-62534449
邮政编码：100871　　　　　　　　　　　 市场营销部电话：010-62750672
电子邮箱：evalee1770@sina.com　　　　　外语编辑部电话：010-62754382

目　录

Unit 1　Creation ··· (1)
　　Text 1　Pan-gu Creating the World ································· (1)
　　Text 2　Nüwa(女娲) and the Creation of Humans ················· (4)
　　Text 3　Situational Dialogue: The Four Supernatural Beasts in Ancient China ······ (9)
　　Text 4　Lecture on Chinese Creation Myths ······················ (12)

Unit 2　Philosophy ·· (24)
　　Text 1　Taoism and Confucianism — Major Chinese Philosophies ······ (24)
　　Text 2　Three Fables in *Zhuangzi* ································ (26)
　　Text 3　Situational Dialogue: About the *Book of Changes* (*The I Ching*) ······ (30)
　　Text 4　An Introduction to the "Hundred Schools of Thought" (诸子百家) ······ (32)

Unit 3　Language and Literature ··· (43)
　　Text 1　*Romance of the Three Kingdoms* ······················· (43)
　　Text 2　Poetry of the Tang Dynasty ······························· (45)
　　Text 3　Situational Dialogue: About *Journey to the West* ···· (48)
　　Text 4　Lecture: An Introduction to Traditional Chinese Literature in Part ····· (50)

Unit 4　Education in Ancient China ····································· (58)
　　Text 1　History of Ancient Chinese Education ··················· (58)
　　Text 2　Confucian Educational Theory ····························· (61)
　　Text 3　Situational Dialogue: On Chinese Imperial Examination ······ (65)
　　Text 4　An Introduction to China Ancient Academies (书院) ···· (68)

Unit 5　Science and Technology ··· (76)
　　Text 1　The Four Great Inventions ································· (76)

1

Text 2　Shen Kuo and *Dream Pool Essays* ……………………………… (80)
Text 3　Situational Dialogue: Xu Guangqi ……………………………… (83)
Text 4　An Introduction to Zhaozhou Bridge ………………………… (85)

Unit 6　Traditional Customs ………………………………………………… (94)

Text 1　Traditional Marriage Rituals ……………………………………… (94)
Text 2　Traditional Chinese Mascots (吉祥物) …………………………… (96)
Text 3　A Situational Dialogue on Fengshui ……………………………… (99)
Text 4　An Introduction to Traditional Chinese Zodiac (生肖) ………… (101)

Unit 7　Beijing in History ………………………………………………… (108)

Text 1　A Brief History of Beijing ………………………………………… (108)
Text 2　Walls and Gates of Beijing ………………………………………… (111)
Text 3　Situational Dialogue: About the Forbidden City ………………… (114)
Text 4　A Tour guide to Beijing's Hutong and Siheyuan ………………… (116)

Unit 8　Leisure ……………………………………………………………… (126)

Text 1　Tea Culture ………………………………………………………… (126)
Text 2　Traditional Music ………………………………………………… (128)
Text 3　Situational Dialogue: About Go (围棋) ………………………… (132)
Text 4　An Introduction to Chinese Calligraphy ………………………… (133)

Unit 9　Virtues ……………………………………………………………… (140)

Text 1　The Five Constant Virtues ………………………………………… (140)
Text 2　Women of Ancient China ………………………………………… (142)
Text 3　Situational Dialogue: About Filial Piety in China ……………… (146)
Text 4　An Introduction to Four Gentlemen in Plants …………………… (148)

Unit 10　National Treasures ……………………………………………… (157)

Text 1　Dunhuang Mogao Grottoes ……………………………………… (157)
Text 2　Tang Tri-Colored Glazed Pottery ………………………………… (160)
Text 3　Situational Dialogue: Face-Changing in Sichuan Opera ……… (164)
Text 4　*The Qingming Festival by the Riverside* ……………………… (167)

Unit 1

Creation

导 读

本单元旨在通过对中国古代神话及相关知识的介绍，使学生了解中国神话对人类起源的贡献，盘古如何开天辟地，女娲如何造人，何为四大神兽，中国神话故事特点等知识，并运用所学中国神话知识及相关的英语表达方式进行跨文化交流，弘扬中华文化。

Before You Start

While you are preparing for this unit, consider what you know about the following questions:
1. How much do you know about the Pan-gu and Nüwa legends?
2. What do you know about the Four Supernatural Beasts in ancient China?
3. What are the specific features of Chinese Mythology?

Section A Reading and Writing

Text 1 Pan-gu Creating the World

All human societies tell stories of how the world began. Such stories are almost infinitely varied in detail, but they tend to include some basic themes. Many accounts begin with earth, or with earth retrieved(取来) from water. In some of them gods and people and animals emerge from the earth (just as plants still do). ① In others the process begins when a creature, such as a crab or tortoise, dives into a primeval ocean and brings up a small piece of earth from which the universe is created. The mythology in China begins with the splitting of a cosmic(宇宙的) egg into half and Pan-gu is the creator of the universe.

Pan-gu creating the World

In the beginning, the heavens and earth were still one and all was chaos(混沌). The universe was like a big black egg, carrying Pan-gu inside itself. The chaos raged on and on — both *yin* and *yang* were mixed together. All the opposites were writhing(盘绕) together, male and female, cold and hot, wet and dry, dark and light. After 18 thousand years, Pan-gu woke from a long sleep. He felt suffocated and began to kick and knock around until he broke the shell and stuck out his head and upper body. He looked around and still saw nothing but darkness. So he took up a broad ax and wielded(挥) it with all his might to crack open the egg. The light, clear part of it floated up and formed the heavens, while the cold, turbid(混浊的) matter stayed below to form earth. Pan-gu stood in the middle, his head touching the sky, his feet planted on the earth. ② Fearing that the sky and the earth would come together and form the chaotic darkness again, Pan-gu decided to stay between the sky and the earth until the world became permanently separate.

The heavens and the earth then began to grow at a rate of ten feet per day, and Pan-gu grew along with them. ③ After another 18 thousand years, the sky was higher, the earth thicker, and Pan-gu stood between them like a pillar 9 million *li* in height so that they would never join again. Time rolling by, Pan-gu had grown old and tired and was too exhausted to stand and grow anymore. At last, he wanted to lie down and sleep. Then one day he suddenly dropped to the ground and fell into a sleep from which he never woke. As he died, the parts of his body became the elements of nature. His breath became the wind and clouds, his voice the rolling thunder. One eye became the sun and the other the moon. His body and limbs turned to five big mountains and his blood formed the roaring water. His veins became far-stretching roads and his muscles fertile lands. The innumerable stars in the sky came from his hair and beard, and flowers and trees from his skin and the fine hairs on his body. His marrow(骨髓) turned to jades and pearls. His sweat flowed like the good rain and sweet dew that nurtured all things on earth. His tears flowed to make rivers and the radiance of his eyes turned into thunder and lightning. One version of the legend has it that the fleas and lice(虱子) on his body became the ancestors of mankind.

The Pan-gu story has become firmly fixed in Chinese tradition. ④ There is even an idiom relating to it: "Since Pan-gu created earth and the heavens," meaning "for a very long time."(576 words)

(Based on http://www.historyworld.net/wrldhis/PlainTextHistories.asp?ParagraphID=bjt)

Unit 1

Creation

Words and Expressions for Pan-gu Creating the World
盘古开天辟地相关英语词汇和表达方式

cosmic	*adj.* 宇宙的
the creator of the universe	宇宙始祖
the heavens and earth were still one and all was chaos	天地合一，万物混沌
writhe	*vt./vi.* 盘绕、扭曲、扭动
suffocate	*v.* 窒息、使窒息、呼吸困难
wield	*vt.* 使用、行使、挥舞
turbid	*adj.* 混浊的
his head touching the sky, his feet planted on the earth	顶天立地
a pillar 9 million *li* in height	九百万里高柱
the rolling thunder	雷霆
roaring	*adj.* 喧闹的、咆哮的、狂风暴雨的
innumerable	*adj.* 无数的、数不清的
marrow	*n.* 骨髓
radiance	*n.* 光辉、发光、容光焕发
flea	*n.* 跳蚤
louse (*pl.* lice)	*n.* 虱子

Difficult Sentences

① In others the process begins when a creature, such as a crab or tortoise, dives into a primeval ocean and brings up a small piece of earth from which the universe is created.
其他关于世界起源的传说通常是诸如螃蟹或乌龟之类的动物潜入原始海洋，带出一块泥土，世界从此开始了。

② Fearing that the sky and the earth would come together and form the chaotic darkness again, Pan-gu decided to stay between the sky and the earth until the world became permanently separate.
由于担心天地重新合一，再现混沌漆黑，盘古决定屹立于天地之间直到天地永久分开。

③ After another 18 thousand years, the sky was higher, the earth thicker, and Pan-gu stood between them like a pillar 9 million *li* in height so that they would never join again.
又过了一万八千年，天空越来越高，大地越来越厚，盘古屹立于天地之间宛如一根九百万里长的擎天柱，从此天地永不相接。

④ There is even an idiom relating to it: "Since Pan-gu created earth and the heavens," meaning "for a very long time."
甚至产生相关习语,如"自盘古开天辟地以来",意为"很久很久以前"。

Text 2　Nüwa(女娲) and the Creation of Humans

A. For many years the world was a very beautiful place but also lonely; there were no people. The half-dragon goddess Nüwa was born after Pan-gu died, from part of the mixture of *yin* and *yang* that he had separated.

B. She decided to create humans to have some other beings to talk to and share ideas with, but mostly just to love. Nüwa went down to the edge of the Yellow River where there were vast, soft mud banks. She began forming figures out of clay. She decided that it would be much more practical for her creations to have legs instead of a dragon tail, thus her humans were not made in her image.

C. ① No sooner had she set the first little mud man on the ground than he started to jump, and dance and sing. He began to speak. "Look at me!" Nüwa was delighted and began making more and more humans. She made hundreds and hundreds of mud humans, but soon realized that it

Nüwa creating human beings

would take centuries for her to make enough people to fill the vast earth completely. Nüwa grabbed hold of a muddy stick and flung drops of mud across the land. As the sun dried each drop, it became a new man or woman.

D. Some say that these humans were the less intelligent ones. Those formed by Nüwa's own hands became great leaders. She told them to go and populate the earth. As they grew, she loved them and protected them, and was revered as the mother of all humans.

E. Nüwa was not just the creator of humans, but the great protector of people. ② In ancient times, the four corners of the sky collapsed and the world with its nine regions split open. The sky could not cover all the things under it, nor could the Earth carry all the things on it. A great fire raged and would not die out; a fierce flood raced about and could not be checked. Savage beasts devoured innocent people; vicious birds preyed on the weak and old.

F. Then Nüwa melted rocks of five colors and used them to mend the cracks in the sky. She supported the four corners of the sky with the legs she had cut off from a giant turtle. She killed the black dragon to save the people and blocked the flood with the ashes of reeds.

Unit 1
Creation

G. Thus the sky was mended, its four corners lifted, the flood tamed, the world pacified, and harmful birds and beasts killed, and the innocent people were able to live on the square Earth under the dome of the sky. It was a time when birds, beasts, insects and snakes no longer used their claws or teeth or poisonous stings, for they did not want to catch or eat weaker things.

H. Nüwa's deeds benefited the heavens above and the Earth below. Her name was remembered by later generations and her light shone on every creation. ③Now she was traveling on a thunder-chariot drawn by a two-winged dragon and two green hornless dragons, with auspicious objects in her hands and a special mattress underneath, surrounded by golden clouds, a white dragon leading the way and a flying snake following behind. ④Floating freely over the clouds, she took ghosts and gods to the ninth heaven and had an audience with the Heavenly Emperor at Ling Men, where she rested in peace and dignity under the emperor. ⑤She never boasted of her achievements, nor did she try to win any renown; she wanted to conceal her virtues, in line with the ways of the universe. (608 words)

Nüwa repairing the cracked heaven

(Based on http://www.geocities.ws/imortakarma/stories.htm)

Words and Expressions for the Legend of Nüwa
女娲传说相关英语词汇和表达方式

half-dragon goddess	人首蛇身女神
grab hold of	抓取、紧握
be revered as the mother of all humans	被尊称为人类之母神
the creator of humans	人类始祖
the four corners of the sky	四极
the world with its nine regions	九州
collapse	v. 倒塌、瓦解
rage	vi. 大怒、发怒;肆虐
race about	乱窜、来回奔走
savage beasts	猛兽
devour	vt. 吞食、毁灭

innocent people	颛民
vicious birds	鸷鹰
prey on	捕食；掠夺
melted rocks of five colors	五彩熔石
legs from a giant turtle	鳌足
black dragon	黑龙
blocked the flood with the ashes of reeds	积芦灰，以止淫水
tame	vt. 驯养、制服
pacify	vt. 使平静、安慰、平定
live on the square Earth	背方州
under the dome of the sky	抱圆天
chariot	战车
a two-winged dragon	应龙
green hornless dragons	青虬
a white dragon	白螭
the ninth heaven	九天

Difficult Sentences

① No sooner had she set the first little mud man on the ground than he started to jump, and dance and sing.

第一个小泥人往地下一放就活了，围着女娲又唱又跳。

② In ancient times, the four corners of the sky collapsed and the world with its nine regions split open.

往古之时，四极废，九州裂。

③ Now she was traveling on a thunder-chariot drawn by a two-winged dragon and two green hornless dragons, with auspicious objects in her hands and a special mattress underneath, surrounded by golden clouds, a white dragon leading the way and a flying snake following behind.

女娲乘雷车，服驾应龙，骖青虬，援绝瑞，席萝图，黄云络，前白螭，后奔蛇。

［该句的意思是：女娲以雷电为车，应龙居中驾辕，青虬（音 qiu）配以两旁，她手持稀奇的瑞玉，铺上带有图案的车垫席，上有黄色的彩云缭绕，前面由白螭开道，后有腾蛇簇拥追随。］

④ Floating freely over the clouds, she took ghosts and gods to the ninth heaven and had an audience with the Heavenly Emperor at Ling Men, where she rested in peace and dignity under the emperor.

浮游逍遥，道鬼神，登九天，朝帝于灵门，宓穆休于太宜之下。

（该句的意思是：她悠闲遨游，鬼神为她引导，上登九天，在灵门朝见天帝，安详静穆地在大道太祖那里休息。）

⑤ She never boasted of her achievements, nor did she try to win any renown; she wanted to conceal her virtues, in line with the ways of the universe.

女娲不彰其功，不扬其声，隐真人之道，以从天地之固然。

（该句的意思是：女娲从来不标榜炫耀自己的功绩，从来不张扬彰显自己的名声，她隐藏起自己的真人之道，以遵从天地自然之道。）

Exercises

Task 1 Thinking and Judging

Directions: *Read Text 1 and judge whether the following statements are true (T), false (F) or not given (NG).*

True   if the statement agrees with the information mentioned in the passage
False if the statement contradicts the information mentioned in the passage
Not Given if there is no information on this in the passage

( ) (1) Before the creation of the universe, everything was in chaos and there were no heavens and earth as well as *yin* and *yang*.
( ) (2) It might have taken over 18 thousand years before Pan-gu came out from the black egg where he slept.
( ) (3) Pan-gu came out of the egg shell naked and howling.
( ) (4) Pan-gu decided to stay between the sky and the earth for the reason that he could grow larger and more powerful.
( ) (5) After 36 years' living, Pan-gu died due to the age and exhaustion.

Task 2 Reading and Matching

Directions: *Read Text 1 again about the creation of elements of nature, and match the following items.*

Organs of Pan-gu	Creations
A. Breath	i. Rolling thunder
B. Two Eyes	ii. The sun and the moon
C. Radiance of his eyes	iii. Jade and pearls
D. His hair and beard	iv. Rain and dew
E. His veins	v. Flowers and trees
F. His marrow	vi. Rivers
G. His body and limbs	vii. Human beings

Organs of Pan-gu	Creations
H. Fleas and lice on his body	viii. Water
I. His tears	ix. Roads
J. His muscles	x. Lands
K. His blood	xi. Five big mountains
L. His voice	xii. The stars
M. His skin and the fine hairs	xiii. Thunder and lighting
N. His sweat	xiv. Wind and clouds
Answers:	

Task 3 Reading Comprehension

Directions: *Read Text 2 and answer the following questions by selecting one correct answer from A, B, C, or D for each question.*

(1) Nüwa created human beings for the reason that _____
   A. she was goddess.　　　　B. she was Pan-gu's daughter.
   C. she felt lonely.　　　　D. she was lovable.

(2) Which of the following about Nüwa's creating human beings is NOT true?
   A. She made man out of yellow clays.
   B. She made more practical legs for humans.
   C. She formed man not in her own image.
   D. She created human beings all by her own hands.

(3) Which of the following has the same meaning as the underlined word "checked" in Paragraph E?
   A. David Smith was about to have his state of health checked by his private surgeon.
   B. Effective measures should be taken to check the spread of bird flu.
   C. All the luggage should be checked before entering the highly secured municipal tower.
   D. All the figures are checked carefully before they are handed in.

(4) Nüwa fixed the collapsed sky through the following measures except _____
   A. cutting the legs off from a giant turtle.
   B. melting rocks of five colors.
   C. killing the black dragon and blocking the flood.
   D. supporting the four corners of the sky.

(5) Which of the following cannot be inferred from the last paragraph?
   A. Nüwa was the wife of the Heavenly Emperor.
   B. Nüwa was a goddess, a symbol of good omen.

C. Nüwa was a selfless goddess.

D. Nüwa's deeds greatly benefited later generations.

Task 4 Researching and Writing

Issue Topic: As we know, the love story of "The Cowherd and the Girl Weaver" is popular with Chinese people, who celebrate it on the seventh day in the seventh month in Chinese lunar calendar unofficially as Chinese Valentine's Day or Double Seventh. Some Chinese scholars try to advise the official government to name it as a national Valentine's day in order to protect traditional Chinese culture. Some refute that as globalization goes faster, China should follow the tradition of western Valentine's celebration on February 14th.

Directions: *Write a 200-word response in which you discuss the extent to which you agree or disagree with the recommendation and explain your reasoning for the position you take. In developing and supporting your position, describe specific circumstances in which adopting the recommendation would or would not be advantageous and explain how these examples support your opinion.*

 vs

Section B Listening and Speaking

Text 3 Situational Dialogue: The Four Supernatural Beasts in Ancient China

Listen to a conversation between a student and a professor discussing Chinese Astrology.

(*P: Peter Cooper, a foreign student studying in Peking University; W: Professor Wang studying Chinese Astrology in Peking University.*)

P: Well, Professor Wang. You just mentioned the four supernatural beasts. They are Green Loong (or Azure Dragon), White Tiger, Zhuque (or the Vermilion Bird) and Xuanwu (or the Black Tortoise), and they have boundless supernatural powers in legend in China's ancient times. What makes them special?

W: ①Interestingly, these four mythological creatures are believed to be the Four Symbols in the Chinese constellations. Each of them represents a direction and a season, and each has its own individual characteristics and origins.

Four Supernatural Beasts

P: That's amazing. Could you tell me in detail about each creature?

W: Sure. Loong, the most inviolable beast, is the emperor's symbol and the representative in the East. There are many legends about Loong in China. By the way, the correct translation should be "Loong" rather than "dragon".

P: Shouldn't Chinese Loong and dragon be the same?

W: No. Absolutely not. In fact, Chinese Loong is totally different from Western dragon. Chinese Loong is a combination of several auspicious animals and it can fly without wings. In contrast, a western dragon looking like a winged dinosaur can fly with its wings and spring fire from its mouth. Besides, people believe Chinese Loong is a positive imaginary creature bringing harvest. But in the west, a dragon is thought to be a negative imaginary image, a violent evil and the embodiment of Satan. In China, people also regard those who are wise and brave as the sons of Chinese Loong, and government officials wear clothes embroidered with Chinese Loong. However, a western dragon can be referred to a person who is violent, combative or very strict.

P: I see. What about White Tiger? As far as I understand, White Tiger and Loong are a pair of best partners. Tiger is regarded as the king of all animals in China.

W: Exactly! During the Han Dynasty, people believed the tiger to be the king of all beasts. Since then, the tiger has been regarded as the King of the beasts for it has a strong appearance and can counteract evil force. ②In the ancient times of China, White Tiger had the supernatural power that dispeled evil spirits and calamity, and prayed for the bumper harvest, getting wealth, getting love etc.

P: But why is the tiger called White Tiger instead of Green Tiger?

W: According to Chinese legends, the tiger's tail would turn into white when it reached the age of 500 years. Thus the white tiger became a kind of mythological creature. It was also said that the white tiger would only appear when the emperor ruled with absolute virtue, or if there was peace throughout the world. Because the color white of the Chinese five elements also represents the west, the white tiger thus becomes a mythological guardian of the west.

P: That's interesting. Now let's talk about Zhuque. Is its direction south or north?

W: Zhuque represents south. It is also known as the Phoenix. The body of Zhuque is the red-like fire and its rebirth can be seen in fire. So it's named Fire Phoenix as well.

P: Does it have any special features?

W: It is believed to be an elegant and noble bird in both appearance and behavior. However, one thing should be noted that it's very selective in what it eats and where it perches(栖息), with its feathers in many different hues of vermilion(朱红色). According to ancient record, the phoenix is a kind of beautiful bird which becomes the queen of the birds due to its wonderful song and beautiful appearance. It can bring good luck to human world. Loong is male and the phoenix is female. Loong matches with the phoenix. There is a kind of legend that "It is very auspicious that Loong appears with the phoenix together" among the Chinese people.

P: The last supernatural beast is Xuanwu. What specific characteristics does it have?

W: Xuanwu, the representative in the North, is made up of tortoise and snake. It is told that there was a kind of tortoise augury(占卜仪式) in China's ancient fortune-telling skill. ③The so-called tortoise augury is to let the tortoise go to the dark hell and ask the ancestry questions, and then brings the answers back, which were shown to common people in divine form.

P: Bravo(妙啊)! How profound and brilliant Chinese culture is. Can all these four supernatural beasts still be seen in China?

W: China's ancient astrology believed Green Loong, White Tiger, Zhuque, Xuanwu, the four supernatural beasts suitable to guard heavenly palace, for they can counteract evil force. So, their images often appear on imperial palaces, hall doors, city gates or other important buildings in China's ancient times.

P: I'm really eager for a field study. In this way, we can understand them better.

W: That's true. I hope someday you can see these images when you visit the Forbidden City, and the Summer Palace.

P: Thank you, Professor Wang. I can't wait to see them with my own eyes. (860 words)

(Based on http://www.historyworld.net/wrldhis/PlainTextHistories.asp?ParagraphID=bjt)

Words and Expressions for Four Supernatural Beasts in Ancient China
中国四大神兽相关英语词汇和表达方式

Green Loong (or Azure Dragon)	青龙
White Tiger	白虎
Zhuque (or the Vermilion Bird)	朱雀
Xuanwu (or the Black Tortoise)	玄武
Four Symbols	四象
Chinese constellations	星宿

inviolable	adj. 神圣的
embodiment	n. 体现、化身
Satan	n. 撒旦(魔鬼)
embroider	v. 刺绣、装饰
combative	adj. 好战的、好事的
counteract	vt. 抵消、中和、阻碍
dispel	v. 驱赶
calamity	n. 灾难
guardian	n. 守护神
perch	vt. 栖息
vermilion	n. 朱红色
auspicious	adj. 吉兆的、吉利的
augury	n. 占卜仪式
fortunetelling	adj. 算命的
implement	n. 工具,器具

Difficult Sentences

① Interestingly, these four mythological creatures are believed to be the Four Symbols in the Chinese constellations. Each of them represents a direction and a season, and each has its own individual characteristics and origins.
有趣的是这四神兽对应着中国星宿中的四象,有着自己的方位和节气,各具特点和起源。

② In the ancient times of China, White Tiger had the supernatural power that dispeled evil spirits and calamity, and prayed for the bumper harvest, getting wealth, getting love etc.
在中国古代,白虎具有许多神奇的能力,它能驱邪避灾,还能带来丰收、财富和爱情。

③ The so-called tortoise augury is to let the tortoise go to the dark hell and ask the ancestry, and then brings the answers back, which were shown to common people in divine form.
所谓的神龟占卜就是派一只神龟到地府去询问祖先,然后把答案带回来,之后再以占卜的形式告知老百姓。

Text 4 Lecture on Chinese Creation Myths

Good morning and welcome to Chinese mythology course. The purpose of this course is to examine China's rich repository(宝库) of myths from a socio-historical perspective and to consider their cultural significance in both ancient and contemporary contexts. In this course, I'll introduce to you a select list of Chinese myths, both well-known and lesser-known ones, and invite you to compare China's mythological tradition with that of other ancient civilizations such as Greece, Scandinavia and Native America. Along the way, you'll be encouraged to examine various Chinese myths from different aspects and contemplate(思考) on their roles within the development of Chinese cultural identity. ①In the end, this course, I hope, will lead you to consider the role of myths in both ancient times and today's modernizing society as well as the way in the changing interpretation of specific mythological motifs which reflect the changes in cultural values.

Fuxi

Our topic today is on the Features of Chinese Mythology. Let me share with you some special features of Chinese Mythology that scholars and critics have agreed on.

1. Mythical stories are entwined with history. The history of the long period before recorded history is partly based on legend, which is interwoven with mythology. Such ancient heroes and leaders as Fuxi, Shennong, Huangdi (the Yellow Emperor) and Yu are both historical figures and important characters in mythical stories.

2. They sing the praises of labor and creation. They extol(赞美) perseverance and self-sacrifice. One typical example is the story of Gun(鲧) and Yu(禹) trying to tame the floods. Gun steals the "growing earth" from the Heavenly God with which to stop the floods, but the God has him killed. Out of his belly Yu is born, who continues his cause. ②Yu goes through countless hardships, remains unmarried until he is thirty, and leaves his wife only four days after their wedding to fight the floods, and finally brings them under control.

Shennong

Huangdi or Yellow Emperor

3. They praise rebellion against oppression. One such story is about a boy whose eyebrows are one foot apart. Ganjiang(干将), who is good at making swords, is killed by the king of Chu. His son Chi(赤) is determined to take revenge. For this he kills himself so that a friend may take his head to see the king and then kill him.

4. They eulogize the yearning for true love. "The Cowherd and the Girl Weaver"(牛郎织女) is certainly one of China's earliest love stories. Many of the mythical stories written by intellectuals tell stories of how men and goddesses, fox fairies or ghost women love each other passionately and sincerely. Such stories reflect, in an indirect way, the yearning for true love although it is stifled by feudal ethical codes.

The Cowherd and the Girl Weaver

5. They encourage good deeds and warn against sin. This is an important theme of the mythical stories produced after the Wei and Jin Dynasties. Their writers might have been motivated by Confucian teachings about humanity and righteousness, and the Buddhist tenet(教义) that good will be rewarded with good and evil repaid with evil.

③ All these features add up, perhaps, to one prevailing characteristic: China's mythical stories, either those created by the primitive people or those written by later scholars, are full of human feelings. Gods, ghosts, foxes and spirits are commonly described as living things with human qualities and human feelings. Chinese inventors of myths describe gods the way they describe man, or treat them as if they were human, and endow them with human nature.

④ There are also stories that try to illustrate fatalism(宿命论), reincarnation(转世说，轮回) and all sorts of feudal ethical principles. This is only natural, because literary works inevitably reflect the beliefs of the age in which they are produced. (626 words)

(Based on http://www.chinavista.com/experience/myth/myth.html)

Words and Expressions for the Lecture on Chinese Creation Myths
中国创世神话相关英语词汇和表达方式

China's rich repository of myths	丰富的中国神话传说
socio-historical perspective	社会历史角度
Scandinavia	n. 斯堪的纳维亚（半岛）
contemplate on	冥思、沉思
strenuous	adj. 艰苦的、费力的
entwine	vt. 使缠绕
interweave	vt. 使交织
tame	vt. 驯养、制服
yearn for	渴望
The Cowherd and the Girl Weaver	牛郎织女
be stifled by	被扼杀、禁止
righteousness	n. 正义、正直、公正
Buddhist tenet	佛教教义
Good will be rewarded with good and evil repaid with evil	善有善报，恶有恶报
add up	把……加起来
prevailing	adj. 流行的、占优势的
fatalism	n. 宿命论
reincarnation	n. 转世说，轮回

Difficult Sentences

① In the end, this course, I hope, will lead you to consider the role of myths in both ancient times and today's modernizing society as well as the way in the changing interpretation of specific mythological motifs which reflect the changes in cultural values.
最后，我希望本课程能引领大家思考神话在古代和现代化社会中的作用，以及如何诠释一些具体反映文化价值取向变化的神话主题。

② Yu goes through countless hardships, remains unmarried until he is thirty, and leaves his wife only four days after their wedding to fight the floods, and finally brings them under control.
禹历经无数艰辛，直到30岁才结婚，婚后四天即离家去治水，最终成功地控制了洪灾。

③ All these features add up, perhaps, to one prevailing characteristic: China's mythical stories, either those created by the primitive people or those written by later scholars, are full of human feelings.

或许从以上的特点中可以归纳出一个广为认可的特征：中国的神话故事，无论是古人创作还是后世学者所著，都充满着人情味。

④ There are also stories that try to illustrate fatalism(宿命论), reincarnation(转世说，轮回)and all sorts of feudal ethical principles.

此外，还有其他有关宿命论、轮回转世及封建伦理的神话小说。

Exercises

Task 1 Listening and Indicating

Directions: *Listen to the situational dialogue and indicate whether the speakers agree with the following statements. For each sentence, tick in the correct box.*

Reasons	YES	NO
(1) The 4 supernatural beasts have their own directions and seasons.		
(2) Although the Chinese Loong is different from the Western dragon, they have similarity to some extent.		
(3) Green Loong represents the west.		
(4) Tiger has been regarded as the King of the beasts since the Han Dynasty.		
(5) Zhuque is so red that it looks like fire.		
(6) If Zhuque dies, it will live in fire eternally.		
(7) It is a good omen when Loong appears with the phoenix together.		
(8) Xuanwu is usually associated with an augury.		
(9) The 4 supernatural beasts guard common households.		
(10) The images of 4 supernatural beasts can often be seen in imperial palaces, ancient Chinese instruments and graves.		

Task 2 Listening and Summarizing

Directions: *Listen to the situational dialogue again and summarize the differences between the Chinese Loong and the Western dragon mentioned in the discussion. Use NO MORE THAN THREE words for each blank.*

Differences	Chinese Loong	Western dragon
Appearance	(1) It combines _____; (2) It can fly _____.	(1) Resembles _____; (2) Flies _____; (3) _____ from its mouth.

Unit 1 Creation

续表

Differences	Chinese Loong	Western dragon
Embodiment	(1) It's the _____ symbol; (2) It can bring _____; (3) Its image is _____. (4) It's the _____ beast.	(1) It symbolizes _____; (2) Its image is _____.
People's Reactions	(1) The _____ individuals are considered as _____ of Chinese Loong; (2) Clothes _____ Chinese Loong are worn by _____	(1) Western dragon is a _____. (2) The _____, _____ or very strict individuals are usually associated with western dragon.

Task 3 Listening and Answering

Directions: *Listen to the lecture once and answer the following questions.*

(1) What is the purpose of this course? It is aimed to _____.

　　A. explore the cultural significance of affluent Chinese myths

　　B. examine a list of Chinese myths from a socio-historical perspective

　　C. compare China's mythological tradition with that of other ancient civilizations

　　D. study Chinese myths from ecological aspects

(2) The professor mentions Fuxi, Shennong, Huangdi (the Yellow Emperor) and Yu in order to _____.

　　A. refute the popular idea that mythical stories are entwined with history

　　B. support the prevailing thought that mythological stories belong to history

　　C. illustrate the characteristic that mythical stories and history are highly related

　　D. examine the agreed belief that ancient heroes are both historical and important figures

(3) What can be inferred in the story of Gun and Yu?

　　A. Yu is the son of Gun.

　　B. Gun is not happy with the Heavenly God and gets killed.

　　C. They steal the "growing earth" from the Heavenly God.

　　D. They have tremendous fortitude to tame the flood.

(4) In feudal society, true love _____.

　　A. was hard to fulfill by young men and women because they don't love each other deeply

　　B. was suppressed by parents who strictly followed the feudal marriage codes

　　C. was accessible by young men and women because of feudal ethical codes

　　D. was believed to be a day dream because of fox fairies' or ghost women's unrequited love

(5) Which of the following does NOT show that Chinese mythical stories are full of human feelings?

A. The stories depict ghosts, foxes and spirits with human feelings.

B. The Cowherd and the Girl Weaver love each other deeply.

C. Gods are described by Chinese inventors of myths the same way as they describe man.

D. The stories are deeply influenced by Buddhist tenet, fatalism and reincarnation.

Task 4 Listening and Interpreting

Directions: *Listen to the lecture twice and then interpret the following sentences into English by resorting to the original expressions you have learned in the lecture and the words and expressions in the chart.*

(1) 众所周知,记录历史之前,很长一段时间的历史是基于传说。
_____
_____

(2) 许多文人墨客笔下的神话故事讲述着人神之恋的真挚强烈爱情。
_____
_____

(3) 想必儒家的仁慈、正义学说激励着许许多多的神话故事创作者。
_____
_____

(4) 文学作品必然反映作品产生的那个时代的精神面貌。
_____
_____

Translation Practice

Directions: *Translate the following passages into English.*

(1) 根据传说,伏羲生于中国西部,出生之前在其母腹中孕育了12年。伏羲教会了人类打猎、捕鱼、驯养野兽、饲养家禽。伏羲制定了人类的嫁娶制度,教会人们劈柴取火和烹煮食物;他还通过龟背上的裂纹创立了八卦,这些八卦成为后来数学、医学、占卜学和风水的发展基础。此外,伏羲创造了中华民族的图腾龙,被认为是中国历史上第一个真正的统治者。

(2) 画蛇添足 刘向(西汉)

楚有祠者,赐其舍人卮酒。舍人相谓曰:"数人饮之不足,一人饮之有余。请画地为蛇,先成者饮酒。"一人蛇先成,引酒且饮之,乃左手持卮,右手画蛇曰:"我能为之足!"未成,一人之蛇成夺取卮曰:"蛇固无足,子安能为之足?"遂饮其酒。为蛇足者,终亡其酒。

Unit 1
Creation

> 白话译文:
> 古代楚国有个人祭过祖宗以后,赏给来帮忙祭祀的门客一壶酒。门客们互相商量说:"大家一起喝这壶酒不足够,一个人喝它还有剩余。要求大家在地上画蛇,先画好的人喝这壶酒。"一个人最先完成了,拿起酒壶准备饮酒,却左手拿着酒壶,右手画蛇,说:"我能够为它画脚。"他还没有把脚画完,另一个人的蛇画好了,抢过他的酒壶,说:"蛇本来就没有脚,你怎么能给它画脚呢?"话刚说完,就把那壶酒喝完了。那个给蛇画脚的人,最终失掉了那壶酒。

Key to Unit 1 Exercises

Before You Start

1. How much do you know about The Pan-gu Legend and Nuwa Legend?

Possible Version:

Pan-gu is a Chinese mythological figure creating the world. At the very beginning, the universe was like a black egg, where he was born. After cracking open the egg, he stood between the sky and the earth until the world became permanently separate. At last, Pan-gu was too exhausted to stand and grow anymore for he had grown old and tired. As he died, the parts of his body became the elements of nature.

Nuwa was a half-dragon goddess born after Pan-gu died. She is regarded as the creator of human beings. She went down to the edge of the Yellow River where she formed figures out of clay. Besides, she was also the great protector of people for she repaired the wall of heaven and killed the black dragon to save the people and blocked the flood with the ashes of reeds.

2. What do you know about the Four Supernatural Beasts in Ancient China?

Possible Version:

Four supernatural beasts are Green Loong (or Azure Dragon), White Tiger, Zhuque (or the Vermilion Bird) and Xuanwu (or the Black Tortoise) that have boundless supernatural powers in legend in China's ancient times. They are believed to be the Four Symbols in the Chinese constellations. Each one of them represents a direction and a season, and each has its own individual characteristics and origins.

3. What are the specific features of Chinese Mythology?

Possible Version:

Briefly speaking, there are several special features of Chinese Mythology that scholars and critics have agreed on. Firstly, Chinese mythical stories are entwined with history. Secondly, they sing the praises of labor and creation and extol perseverance and self-sacrifice. Besides, they praise rebellion against oppression. Moreover, they eulogize the yearning for true love and encourage good deeds and warn against sin. All these features add up, perhaps, to one prevailing feature: China's mythical stories, either those created by the primitive people or those written by later scholars, are full of human feelings. Additionally, there are mythical stories involving fatalism, reincarnation and all sorts of feudal ethical principles.

Section A Reading and Writing

Text 1 Pan-gu Creating the World

Exercises

Task 1 **Thinking and Judging**
(1) T   (2) T   (3) NG   (4) F   (5) F

Task 2 **Reading and Matching**

Organs of Pan-gu	Creations
A. Breath	i. Rolling thunder
B. Two Eyes	ii. The sun and the moon
C. Radiance of his eyes	iii. Jade and pearls
D. His hair and beard	iv. Rain and dew
E. His veins	v. Flowers and trees
F. His marrow	vi. Rivers
G. His body and limbs	vii. Human beings
H. Fleas and lice on his body	viii. Water
I. His tears	ix. Roads
J. His muscles	x. Lands
K. His blood	xi. Five big mountains
L. His voice	xii. The stars
M. His skin and the fine hairs	xiii. Thunder and lighting
N. His Sweat	xiv. Wind and clouds

Answers: A-xiv; B-ii; C-xiii; D-xii; E-ix; F-iii; G-xi; H-vii; I-vi; J-x; K-viii; L-i; M-v; N-iv

Text 2 Nuwa and the Creation of Humans

Exercises

Task 3 **Reading Comprehension**
(1) C   (2) D   (3) B   (4) C   (5) A

Task 4 **Researching and Writing**
Possible Version:
Nowadays, with the rapid development of economy and the speeding proliferation of

technology, human beings have been freed from the shackles of tedious and laborious physical work and have more time to think about how to enrich the spiritual life. Valentine's celebration is one of the improvements. Some scholars suggest to the official government that the day of the reunion of the Cowherd and the Girl Weaver or Double Seventh should be considered as national Valentine's day in order to protect the traditional Chinese culture, while others advise that China should follow the trend of western Valentine's celebration on February 14th because of the escalating globalization. As far as I'm concerned, the former suggestion is more favorable.

If we nation-widely celebrate Valentine's Day on the Seventh day in the seventh month in Chinese lunar calendar, it will foster a sense of patriotism, protecting our traditional Chinese culture. The love story of "The Cowherd and the Girl Weaver" is popular with Chinese people. This love is sincere and true, which not only encourages the youth to seek the chance to express their love to the loved but also admonish them to cherish the love they have. All Chinese people have the responsibility of protecting our traditional Chinese culture. Besides, although keeping pace with the international trend is significant, still spreading our own culture is equally imperative due to the escalating comprehensive power of China and the massive foreign visitors and students in China. Foreigners come to China in hopes of experiencing more Chinese traditional life styles. Familiar with western Valentine's celebrations on February 14th, they would rather see the special observation spurred by the love story of "The Cowherd and the Girl Weaver".

To sum up, it is imperatively significant to nationally celebrate our Chinese Valentine's Day based on the love story of "The Cowherd and the Girl Weaver".

Section B Listening and Speaking

Text 3   The Four Supernatural Beasts in Ancient China

Exercises

Task 1   **Listening and Indicating**

Reasons	YES	NO
(1) The 4 supernatural beasts have their own directions and seasons.	√	
(2) Although the Chinese Loong is different from the Western dragon, they have similarity to some extent.		√
(3) Green Loong represents the west.		√
(4) Tiger has been regarded as the King of the beasts since the Han Dynasty.	√	

Reasons	YES	NO
(5) Zhuque is so red that it looks like fire.	✓	
(6) If Zhuque dies, it will live in fire eternally.		✓
(7) It is a good omen when Loong appears with phoenix together.	✓	
(8) Xuanwu is usually associated with an augury.	✓	
(9) The 4 supernatural beasts guard common households.		✓
(10) The images of 4 supernatural beasts can often be seen in imperial palace, ancient Chinese instruments and graves.	✓	

Task 2   Listening and Summarizing

Differences	Chinese Loong	Western dragon
Appearance	(1) It combines several propitious animals; (2) It can fly without wings.	(1) Resembles a winged dinosaur; (2) Flies with its wings; (3) Springs fire from its mouth.
Embodiment	(1) It's the emperor's symbol; (2) It can bring harvest; (3) Its imaginary is positive. (4) It's the most inviolable beast.	(1) It symbolizes Satan; (2) Its image is negative.
People's Reactions	(1) The wise and gentle individuals are considered as the son of Chinese Loong; (2) Clothes embroidered with Chinese Loong are worn by Government officials.	(1) Western dragon is a violent evil. (2) The violent, combative or very strict individuals are usually associated with western dragon.

Text 4   Lecture on Chinese Creation Myths

Exercises

Task 3   Listening and Answering
(1) A   (2) C   (3) D   (4) B   (5) D

Task 4   Listening and Interpreting
(1) 众所周知,记录历史之前,很长一段时间的历史是基于传说。
As is known to all, the history of the long period before recorded history is based on legend.

(2) 许多文人墨客笔下的神话故事讲述着人神之恋的真挚热烈。
Many of the mythical stories written by intellectuals tell stories of how men and goddesses love each other passionately and sincerely.

(3) 想必儒家的仁慈、正义学说激励着许许多多的神话故事创作者。
The writers of myths and legends might have been motivated by Confucian teachings about humanity and righteousness.

(4) 文学作品必然反映作品产生的那个时代的精神面貌。
Literary works inevitably reflect the beliefs of the age in which they are produced.

参考译文

(1) Fuxi was born in the west part of China. According to legend, he was carried in his mother's womb for twelve years before birth. He taught people how to hunt, fish, domesticate(驯化) animals and tend their poultry. He instituted(制定)marriage system and taught people how to devise tools to split wood, kindle(点燃) fire and cook food. He devised the Eight Trigrams(八卦), which was based upon markings on tortoise shells. These trigrams served as the basis for later development of mathematics, medicine, divination(占卜) and geomancy(风水术). Furthermore, he created the Chinese dragon as the totem of the nation and was considered as the first real ruler in the chinese history.

(2) **The Man Who Draws a Snake and Adds Feet to It**
By Liu Xiang of the Western Han Dynasty

A native of Chu gave his retainers(随从;门客)a pot of wine after worshipping the ancestors. One of the retainers said, "The wine is insufficient for all of us, though too much for one of us. I suggest, therefore, that we draw snakes on the ground, and the one who first finishes drawing the snake will win the pot of wine." When one retainer had completed his drawing, he took the pot and was about to drink. He held it in his left hand and continued to draw with his right hand, saying: "I can add feet to it." While he was adding feet to his snake, another man who had then finished drawing snatched the pot from his hand, claiming: "No snake has feet. How can you add feet to it?" Then he took the wine. The man who added feet to the snake lost his prize at last.

Unit 2

Philosophy

> **导 读**
>
> 本单元旨在简要介绍以儒家、道家为主流的中国传统哲学,让学生在理解哲学思想的基础上学会相关的语言知识,加强对中国哲学脉络的把握,并在对外交流过程中更好地弘扬本民族的思想文化。

Before You Start

While you are preparing for this unit, think about the following questions:

1. What do you know about Chinese philosophies and philosophers? Give some names and terms for example.
2. Do you still remember some famous quotes from Confucius or Lao Tzu? Recite three pieces in Chinese.
3. Do you believe in fortune-telling? How many ways do you know that can tell one's fortune? What are they?

Section A Reading and Writing

Text 1 Taoism and Confucianism — Major Chinese Philosophies

The 6th century B. C. E. was an amazing time of philosophical growth for ancient China. It was during that time that the two most influential spiritual leaders native to China, Lao-tzu and Confucius, are thought to have lived and taught. ①The philosophies that they practiced, Taoism and Confucianism, existed simultaneously in dynastic China, attracting countless numbers of followers over the past 2,500 years.

Lao-tzu and Taoism

Lao-tzu, whose original name was Lao Dan, is believed to be the founder of Taoism. Very little is known of his life; he may not even have existed. It is said that he once took a position as head librarian of the Imperial Archives①. Saddened by society's lack of goodness, Lao-tzu decided to leave civilization and live out the rest of his life in quiet and solitude. Before he left, he wrote down his parting thoughts, which were titled the *Tao Te Ching*②, and became the most important text of Taoism.

According to Taoism, the entire universe and everything in it flow with a mysterious, unknowable force called the Tao. Translated literally as "The Way," the Tao has many different meanings. It is the name that describes ultimate reality. The Tao also explains the powers that drive the universe and the wonder of human nature. Taoists believe that everything is one despite all appearances. Opinions of good and evil or true and false only happen when people forget that they are all one in the Tao.

②Nevertheless, Lao-tzu reminds believers that the Tao is difficult to grasp: *"The Tao that can be spoken is not the true Tao."*

Confucius and Confucianism

The other driving philosophy of dynastic China was created by a politician, educator, and philosopher named Confucius (whose original name was Kong Qiu). Born in 551 B.C.E., Confucius wandered throughout China, first as a government employee, and later as a political advisor to the rulers of the Chou dynasty. In later life, Confucius left politics to teach a small group of students. After his death in 479 B.C.E., the ethics and moral teachings of Confucius were written down by his students to become the *Lun-yü*, or *Analects*. Many of his clever sayings are still followed today.

Learning to be human was the goal of Confucianism. ③According to Confucius, each person should act with virtue in all social matters to ensure order and unity, bringing good to family, state and the whole world. Confucian ceremonies contained many rituals based on the Five Classics, especially the *I Ching*, or *Book of Changes*.

However, by far the most influential aspect of Confucianism remains in *The Analects*. It was these sayings of wisdom that made Confucianism the social philosophy of China from the Han Dynasty in the 2nd Century B.C.E. until the end of dynastic rule in the early 20th Century C.E.

---

① The Imperial Archives：指的是当时周王朝的国家藏书机构。据《史记》记载，老子做过周朝"守藏室之史"，相当于王室藏书馆的馆长。

② *Tao Te Ching*,《道德经》，又称《老子》、《道德真经》、《五千言》，是我国首部完整的哲学著作。分上下两篇，上篇《德经》、下篇《道经》，语言简约玄妙，以"道法自然"、"清静无为"的处世哲学、"物极必反"、"福祸相倚"的辩证法思想成为中国文化根基的重要组成部分。后世对《道德经》的文本进行过多次修订。

Rival Philosophies

Taoism and Confucianism have lived together in China for well over 2,000 years. Confucianism deals with social matters, while Taoism concerns itself with the search for meaning of existence. ④They share common beliefs about man, society, and the universe, although these notions were around long before either philosophy. Both began as philosophies, each later taking on religious overtones. Regardless of the disagreements between Lao-tzu and Confucius, both Taoism and Confucianism have served as spiritual guides. They have led China through the peaks and valleys of its vast history, the longest continuing story on the planet. (542 words)

(Based on http://www.ushistory.org/civ/9 e.asp)

Difficult Sentences

① The philosophies that they practiced, Taoism and Confucianism, existed simultaneously in dynastic China, attracting countless numbers of followers over the past 2,500 years.
他们所实行的哲学,道家思想和儒家思想,在封建时代的中国同时存在,在过去的2500年间吸引了无数的追随者。

② Nevertheless, Lao-tzu reminds believers that the Tao is difficult to grasp: *"the Tao that can be spoken is not the true Tao."*
然而,老子提醒信徒们,"道"是很难把握的:"道可道,非常道"。("道可道,非常道"是《道德经》的第一句,有多种理解与译法。本文中的理解是最常见的一种,即:能够被言说的道并不是真正的道。)

③ According to Confucius, each person should act with virtue in all social matters to ensure order and unity, bringing good to family, state and the whole world.
孔子认为,在所有的社会事务上,每个人都应该依礼行事,以保证秩序和统一,给家庭、国家和世界带来祥和。(这是儒家"修身、齐家、治国、平天下"的理想。)

④ They share common beliefs about man, society, and the universe, although these notions were around long before either philosophy.
他们对于人、社会和宇宙有着共同的看法,虽然这些理念在这两种哲学思想产生之前就早已存在了。(道家、儒家思想都以《周易》为基础,《周易》中的阴阳相克相生的思想早在远古时期就已通过八卦图的形式展现,远早于道家、儒家哲学的流传。)

Text 2　Three Fables in *Zhuangzi*

Among all the Chinese thinkers from antiquity (古代) onward, Zhuangzi (whose original name was Zhuang Zhou), an early Taoist, is fond of using fables to explain his ideas. His writing style is beautifully unique, with vivid imagination and profound thoughts that are not clearly demonstrated in plain words. Hence it often leads to a diversity of interpretations. ① A serious reader of the *Book of Zhuangzi*① tends to be inspired each time when scrutinizing（细读）it and consequently comes out with new findings in accordance with one's lived experience, individual perspective, and ever deepened understanding of human existence in itself.

Let us look into three fables among many others.

1. Travel in Boundless Freedom（逍遥游②）

In the Northern Ocean there is a fish, by the name of Kun, which is many thousand miles in size. This fish metamorphoses（变形）into a bird by the name of Peng, whose back is many thousand miles in breadth. When the bird rouses itself and flies, its wings obscure

the sky like clouds. When Peng is moving to the Southern Ocean, it flaps along the water for 3,000 miles. ②Then it ascends on a whirlwind up to a height of 90,000 miles, for a flight of six months' duration. With the blue sky above, and no obstacle on the way, it mounts upon wind and starts for the south.

A cicada（蝉）and a young dove laugh at Peng, saying: "When we make an effort, we fly up to the trees. Sometimes, not able to reach, we fall to the ground midway. What is the use of going up 90,000 miles in order to fly toward the south?"

A quail（鹌鹑）also laughs at it, saying: "Where is that bird going? I spring up with a bound, and when I have reached no more than a few yards I come down again. I just fly about among the brushwood（矮林）and the bushes. It is also perfect flying…" It is the difference between the great and the small.

2. Zhuang Zhou or a Butterfly?（庄周梦蝶③）

③Once Zhuang Zhou dreamt he was a butterfly, a butterfly flitting and fluttering around, happy with himself and doing as he pleased. He didn't know he was Zhuang Zhou. Suddenly he woke up and there he was, solid and unmistakable Zhuang Zhou. But he didn't know if he was Zhuang Zhou who had dreamt he was

庄周梦蝶图（范曾作）

---

① Zhuangzi：也译作 Chuang-tzu,庄子（公元前 369—前 286），战国时期宋国人，继老子之后道家学说的主要创始人之一。著有《庄子》（又名《南华经》）一书，笔法雄奇，语言瑰丽，成为我国思想性、文学性价值极高的主要典籍。

② 《逍遥游》是《庄子》书中的第一篇（"北冥有鱼，其名为鲲"），译文有删节。

③ "庄周梦蝶"出自《庄子·齐物论》。

a butterfly, or a butterfly dreaming he was Zhuang Zhou. Between Zhuang Zhou and a butterfly there must be some distinction. This is called the Transformation(转化) of Things.

3. An Argument on the Bridge(濠梁之辩①)

Observing the fish in the Hao River from the bridge, Zhuangzi said to Huizi, "The fish are swimming leisurely and cozily; how happy they are!" At that, Huizi asked at once, "You're not a fish and how can you tell they are happy?" Zhuangzi retorted immediately: "You are not me and how can you tell I don't know they're happy?" Huizi argued, "Indeed, I'm not you, nor can I tell; you are not a fish, and you don't either. That's all." Zhuangzi urged, "Please get back to your original question; you asked 'How can you tell the fish are happy?' which indicates that you knew I knew. I knew it on the bridge of the Hao River."

No matter what meanings people may cultivate from these fables, they are able to get hold of the primary message provided they explore along Zhuangzi's path of thought. ④This path winds through all his writings, and reflects his constant preoccupation with(专心于) the Dao(Tao, Way) of attaining spirited liberation and independent personality. These two aspects of the Dao can be identified with the two sides of the same coin termed as absolute freedom. The freedom as such is assumed to enable human fulfillment that is conceived of as the ultimate(终极的) goal for life. All this is largely grounded on a sincere and supra-utilitarian(超越功利的) attitude toward the pursuit of spiritual transcendence(超脱). (681 words)

(Based on a paper entitled "Zhuangzi's Way of Thinking through Fables" by Wang Keping(王柯平). The fables were translated by Burton Watson.)

Difficult Sentences

① A serious reader of the *Book of Zhuangzi* tends to be inspired each time when scrutinizing(细读) it and consequently comes out with new findings in accordance with one's lived experience, individual perspective, and ever deepened understanding of human existence in itself

认真阅读《庄子》的人在每次细读此书时都会得到启示，从而根据自己的生活经历、个人视角以及不断加深的人生体验获得新的发现。

---

① "濠梁之辩"出自《庄子·秋水》，是庄子与惠子的一场著名争辩。惠子，即惠施(公元前390—前317)，战国时期政治家、哲学家，好思辨，是名家思想的开山鼻祖和主要代表人物。

② Then it ascends on a whirlwind up to a height of 90,000 miles, for a flight of six months' duration.

然后它乘着旋风,直上九万里,一飞就是六个月。

③ Once Zhuang Zhou dreamt he was a butterfly, a butterfly flitting and fluttering around, happy with himself and doing as he pleased.

庄周曾梦见自己是一只蝴蝶,一只翩翩飞舞的蝴蝶,逍遥自在,悠然自得。

④ This path winds through all his writings, and reflects his constant preoccupation with the Dao (Tao, Way) of attaining spirited liberation and independent personality.

这条思路贯穿在他所有的文章中,反映了他对于"道"始终一以贯之的言说,目的是实现精神的解放和独立的人格。

Exercises

Task 1 Skimming and Scanning

Directions: *In this part, you will have 10 minutes to go over Text 1 quickly, then answer the following questions.*

For questions 1—7, mark

Y (for YES) if the statement agrees with the information given in the passage;

N (for NO) if the statement contradicts the information given in the passage;

NG (for NOT GIVEN) if the information is not given in the passage.

For questions 8—10, complete the sentences with the information given in the passage.

( ) (1) Lao-tzu and Confucius were both native Chinese philosophers born in the 6th century B.C.E.

( ) (2) Lao-tzu was only a legendary figure who had never really existed.

( ) (3) According to *Tao Te Ching*, all things are one although they look different.

( ) (4) Confucius was not only a philosopher, but a politician and educator.

( ) (5) The book *Analects* was written by Confucius to promote his thought.

( ) (6) Confucius learned much from Lao-tzu and developed his own philosophy.

( ) (7) The main target of Confucianism was learning to get rid of worldly worries.

(8) The most important text of Confucianism is _____.

(9) Confucianism places emphasis on social matters while Taoism on searching for _____.

(10) Although Taoism and Confucianism are different, they have both served as _____ for Chinese people.

Task 2 Translating

Directions: *Translate the following sayings from* The Analects *back into Chinese.*

(1) The Master said, "Is it not a pleasure, having learned something, to try it out at

due intervals? Is it not a joy to have friends come from afar? Is it not gentlemanly not to take offence when others fail to appreciate your abilities?"

(2) The Master said, "A man is worthy of being a teacher who gets to know what is new by keeping fresh in his mind what he is already familiar with."

(3) The Master said, "He who gives no thought to difficulties in the future is sure to be beset by worries much closer at hand."

(4) The Master said, "If one learns from others but does not think, one will be bewildered. If, on the other hand, one thinks but does not learn from others, one will be in peril."

(5) The Master said, "At fifteen I set my heart on learning; at thirty I took my stand; at forty I came to be free from doubts; at fifty I understood the Decree of Heaven; at sixty my ear was attuned; at seventy I followed my heart's desire without overstepping the line."

Task 3   Discussing and Writing

Directions: *Read Text 2 carefully. Consider what Zhuangzi intended to convey in the three fables. Discuss it in class with your classmates and then write an essay with at least 150 words, stating your understanding of these fables as well as Zhuangzi's philosophy.*

Section B Listening and Speaking

Text 3   Situational Dialogue: About the *Book of Changes* (the *I Ching*)

(H: Howard, an American student learning Chinese language and culture in Beijing; L: Liu Lily, a Chinese graduate student majoring in Chinese philosophy. They are in a bookstore.)

L: Hi, Howard, what are you reading?

H: A book about fortune telling by horoscope (星象). Do you believe in it?

L: Sort of. I know I'm a Scorpion (天蝎) and I have read some tips about my horoscope, but I prefer our Chinese way of fortune-telling. It's incredible!

H: Really? Tell me about it.

L: Come here. I'll show you a wonderful book. This one, the *I Ching*, also translated as the *Book of Changes*. It's supposed to be the oldest and greatest book of Chinese culture, providing the most wonderful way of fortune telling.

H: Sounds awesome. What do these signs of lines mean?

L: They are signs of how things happen and change. ① In ancient times, people divided grass sticks to tell how these signs go; nowadays people toss coins to predict their fortune according to the *I Ching*. ② You toss three coins for six times, then you get a hexagram composed of the trigrams (卦) in the *I Ching*, and the book will tell you what this hexagram means in what you want to know. Those who have their fortune told in this way always say things go exactly as it is told.

H: Wow, my head is swirling (晕眩). Horoscope is much easier and simpler than your *Book of Changes*. You are lucky to have such a wonderful book for fortune-telling.

L: Thanks. Actually, the charm of the *I Ching* lies in the very fact that things are always changing, so is one's fortune. What's more, the *I Ching* is far from a fortune book; it serves as the foundation of Chinese philosophy. The *I Ching* is regarded as both a Book of Oracles (占卜) and a Book of Philosophy. ③ At the outset, it was a collection of linear signs to be used as oracles. ④ Philosophically, it is a book written to reveal the patterns (the Tao) of things changing between the heavens, earth and humans, which ancient Chinese philosophers referred to as a whole. It aims to help things flourish (繁荣) and put human affairs in harmony with nature.

H: I wonder who wrote this great book?

L: In Chinese literature four holy men① are cited as the authors of the *I Ching*, namely, Fu-xi(伏羲), King Wên of Zhou(周文王), the Duke of Zhou(周公), and Confucius. ⑤ The authors of the book imitated the innumerable changing things in the cosmos by applying a structure of hexagrams and images based on the observation of natural changes.

H: So many Chinese philosophers wrote it. No wonder it's so profound. I hope someday I can have my fortune told by the *I Ching*.

Eight Trigram Chart (八卦图)

L: It's convenient. I'll introduce an *I Ching* expert for you to consult if you need to.

H: Can't wait. Thanks in advance.

(Based on http://www.iging.com/intro/introduc.htm)

Difficult Sentences

① In ancient times, people divided grass sticks to tell how things went; nowadays people toss coins to predict their fortune according to the *I Ching*.

---

① 传说中《周易》的四位作者,根据《史记》记载,远古的神人伏羲根据河洛之图作八卦图以明天道,到了商朝末年,周文王被商纣王拘禁在羑里,文王将伏羲八卦演变为六十四卦系辞以序人事,其子周公做重卦、爻辞以卜吉凶,而孔子做了阐释《易经》的《易传》(又名《十翼》)以明万理。

古代的时候，人们通过分配草秆的方式来决定这些卦象的排列，现在人们是通过掷硬币的方式来参照《周易》预测命运。

② You toss three coins for six times, then you get a hexagram composed of the six trigrams（卦）in the *I Ching*, and the book will tell you what this hexagram means in what you want to know.

把三个硬币抛六次，得到六道卦线组成的卦图，《周易》里有卦辞会解释这个卦象对于你想知道的事意味着什么。

③ At the outset, it was a collection of linear signs to be used as oracles.

从表面上看，这本书上画了大量用来占卜的横线。

④ Philosophically, it is a book written to reveal the patterns（the Dao）of things changing between the heavens, earth and humans, which ancient Chinese philosophers refer to as a whole.

从哲学意义上说，这本书写来是为了揭示天、地、人之间事物的变化之道，中国古代哲人认为这三者是一个整体。

⑤ The authors of the book imitated the innumerable changing things in the cosmos by applying a structure of hexagrams and images based on the observation of natural changes.

这部书的作者们在观察自然变更的基础上，通过八卦的卦象和图形，效仿宇宙间无数变化的事物。

Text 4　An Introduction to the "Hundred Schools of Thought"（诸子百家）

In the turbulent（动荡不安的）Spring and Autumn Period（770—476 B.C.E.）and Warring States Period（475—221 B.C.E.），many schools of thought were flourishing.

墨子

The four most influential schools of thought that evolved during this period were Confucianism, Taoism, Mohism（墨家）, and Legalism（法家）. There were also other schools like Yin & Yang（阴阳家）, Logicians（名家）, Diplomats（纵横家）and Militarism（兵家）. ①These controversial thoughts intensified activities and debates in the intellectual and ideology system in ancient China and exerted great influence on Chinese culture.

The Mohism founded by Mozi prospered in the latter half of the fifth century B.C.E. It resembles Confucianism in its reverence for humanism. Master Mo① called for a universal love encompassing all

---

① Master Mo：墨子（公元前468—前376），名翟（dí），春秋末战国初期宋国（今河南商丘）人，一说鲁国（今山东滕州）人，是战国时期著名的思想家、教育家、科学家、军事家，墨家学派的创始人，后来其弟子收集其语录，完成《墨子》一书传世，主张"兼爱"、"非攻"。

human beings in equal degree. He suggested a harmonious relationship between people on a reciprocal basis. ②Thus he was an assertor of unionism who suggested a practice of a political relationship of mutual benefit or dependence between states.

The Legalist School sought by every means possible to strengthen the state and increase its military might. It began to take shape late in the fourth century B. C. E. Earlier legalists were Shang Yang① and Li Kui②. Later in the Warring States Period, the most important legalist named Han Fei③ advocated harsh rules and laws. He was born in a rich family in the state of Han. ③In the book *Hanfeizi*, he was bent on organizing society on a rational basis and finding means to strengthen a state agriculturally and militarily. He also advised elaborate means for controlling people's lives and actions through laws and punishments. Han Fei's theory was applied by the state of Qin and played an important role in the unification(统一) of China by Emperor Qin Shihuang.

韩非子

For some other famous schools, the School of Yin-yang was a philosophy that synthesized (合成) the concepts of yin-yang and the Five Elements④; Zou Yan⑤ is considered the founder of this school. The School of Names or Logicians⑥ grew out of Mohism, with a philosophy that focused on definition and logic. The most notable Logician was Gongsun Long⑦. The

---

① Shang Yang：商鞅(公元前395—前338)，战国时代政治家，著名法家代表人物。卫国国君的后裔，故称为卫鞅，后封于商，后人称之商鞅。在秦国执政十九年，以严刑酷法著称，秦国大治，史称商鞅变法。著有《商君书》。

② Li Kui：李悝(公元前455—前395)，战国时魏国人，著名的政治家，法家代表人物，曾任魏国宰相，在魏国变法图强。

③ Han Fei：韩非(公元前281？—前233)，战国末期韩国人(今河南省新郑)，哲学家、思想家、政论家和散文家，法家思想的集大成者，后世称"韩子"或"韩非子"，法家思想的代表人物，著作收录在《韩非子》一书中。曾得秦王嬴政的重用，后死在秦国狱中。

④ the Five Elements：五行，指：金、木、水、火、土。五行是中国古代的一种物质观。多用于哲学、中医学和占卜方面。五行认为大自然由这五种要素构成，这五个要素的盛衰使得大自然产生变化，不但影响到人的命运，同时也使宇宙万物循环不已。

⑤ Zou Yan：邹衍(约公元前305—前240)，战国末期齐国人，阴阳家学派创始者与代表人物。他把春秋战国时期流行的五行说应用到历史观点上，提出"五德始终"的历史观，即整个物质世界是由金、木、水、火、土构成的，事物发展变化是通过五行相克相生来实现的；而人类社会历史的发展是一种客观必然，像自然一样。

⑥ School of Names or Logicians：名家，先秦时期以辩论名实问题为中心的一个思想派别，重视"名"(概念)和"实"(事)的关系的研究。

⑦ Gongsun Long：公孙龙(公元前320—前250)，战国末年赵国人，哲学家，能言善辩，名家离坚白派的代表人物，著有《公孙龙子》一书，提出了"离坚白"、"白马非马"等命题。

School of Diplomacy① specialized in diplomatic politics; Zhang Yi ②and Su Qin③ were representative thinkers. The Miscellaneous School④ integrated teachings from different schools; for instance, Lü Buwei⑤ found scholars from different schools to write a book called *Lüshi Chunqiu*（《吕氏春秋》）cooperatively. This school tried to integrate the merits of various schools and avoid their perceived flaws.

The Hundred Schools of Thought, plus the Buddhist thought⑥ imported from India in around the first century, laid a solid foundation for Chinese philosophy. ④ The thoughts and ideas discussed and refined during this period have profoundly influenced lifestyles and social consciousness up to the present day in China and other East Asian countries. （507 words）

(Based on http://www.chinaculture.org/gb/en_aboutchina/2003-09/24/content_23009.htm)

Difficult Sentences

① These controversial thoughts intensified activities and debates in the intellectual and ideology system in ancient China and exerted great influence on Chinese culture.
这些思想流派颇具争议，推动了中国古代知识界和意识形态领域的活动与辩论，对中国文化产生了重要影响。

② Thus he was an assertor of unionism who suggested a practice of a political relationship of mutual benefit or dependence between states.
他是联合原则的倡导者，主张推行国与国之间互利互惠、相互依赖的政治关系。

③ In the book *Han Fei Zi*, he bent on organizing society on a rational basis and finding means to strengthen their states agriculturally and militarily.
在《韩非子》这本书中，他立志以理性眼光看待社会，寻求途径让自己的国邦在农业和军事上强大起来。

---

① School of Diplomacy：纵横家，出现于战国至秦汉之际，多为策辩之士，可称为中国五千年中最早也最特殊的外交政治家。战国时以从事政治外交活动为主的一派，是诸子百家之一，创始人鬼谷子，杰出代表人物有：苏代、姚贾、苏秦、张仪、公孙衍等。

② Zhang Yi：张仪（？—前309），战国时魏国贵族后裔，著名政治家、外交家和谋略家。他曾两次为秦相，运用连横策略，游说六国分别与秦国结盟。

③ Su Qin：苏秦（？—前317），战国时洛阳人，是与张仪齐名的纵横家。曾身佩六国相印，组织六国君联合抗秦，称为"合纵"。

④ The Miscellaneous School：杂家，中国战国末至汉初的哲学学派。以博采各家之说见长，以"兼儒墨，合名法"为特点，"于百家之道无不贯通"。杂家的代表一是编撰《淮南子》的淮南王刘安，另一是编撰《吕氏春秋》的吕不韦。

⑤ Lü Buwei：吕不韦（？—前235年），战国末期卫国著名商人、政治家、思想家。后为秦国丞相。曾组织门客编写了号称"一字千金"的《吕氏春秋》（又称《吕览》），是杂家思想的代表作。后被迫饮鸩自尽。

⑥ Buddhist thought：佛家思想，又称释家思想，是中国传统哲学思想的组成部分之一。印度佛教于两汉之际传播到中国内地，与儒家、道家思想相印证交融，两千年来对中国文化产生了巨大影响，形成了儒、释、道共存的思想文化积淀。

④ The thoughts and ideas discussed and refined during this period have profoundly influenced lifestyles and social consciousness up to the present day in China and other East Asian countries.

这个时期所讨论和升华的思想和理念至今还深刻影响着中国和其他东亚国家的生活方式和社会意识。

Exercises

Task 1 Listening and Speaking

Directions: *Listen to the dialogue carefully. Discuss with your classmates about the I Ching and answer the following questions.*

(1) What is the English translation of 《易经》 other than the *I Ching*?
(2) What instruments can be used for fortune-telling by the *I Ching*?
(3) Why is the *I Ching* so fascinating?
(4) What is the philosophical significance of the *I Ching*?
(5) Who wrote the *I Ching*?

Task 2 Listening and Blank Filling

Directions: *Listen to An Introduction to the "Hundred Schools of Thought" twice and, combined with the texts in Section A, complete the following table with the missing information about schools of thought and their representatives and masterpieces.*

	School of thought	Representative	Masterpiece
(1)	Confucianism	Confucius	_____
		_____	*Mencius*
(2)	_____	Lao Tzu	_____
		_____	*Zhuangzi*
(3)	_____	Mo Di	*Mozi*
(4)	_____	Han Fei	
(5)	_____	Gongsun Long	*Gongsun Longzi*
(6)	_____	Zou Yan	*Zouzi*
(7)	The School of Diplomacy	_____ , _____	
(8)	The Miscellaneous School	_____	*Lüshi Chunqiu*

Task 3　Making a Short Speech

Directions: *Make a short speech of 5 minutes in class, introducing one of your favorite schools of Chinese thought or ancient Chinese philosophers. You can find more information from books or the Internet to enrich your presentation and use MS PowerPoint to help you during your speech.*

Translation Practice

Directions: *Translate the following passages into English.*

（1）儒家的创始人是孔子(公元前551—前479)，他提出了一套道德规范，基于五种美德：仁、义、礼、智、信。其中"仁"被认为是他的哲学理念的基石，代表着忠诚、孝道(filial piety)、宽容和善良。他还提倡人与人之间和谐相处，按照行为规范标准建立生活社区。他的追随者之一孟子(公元前372—前289)不断地向统治者们游说，试图说服他们修身养德，为人典范，以仁政赢得人民的尊重。

（2）中国哲学有着几千年的历史，其起源可以追溯到《易经》，其中介绍了一些最重要的中国哲学概念。自始至终中国哲学的核心就是对人与社会的现实关注、如何过理想的生活，以及如何去组织社会。伦理(ethics)和政治哲学(political philosophy)常常超越在形而上学(metaphysics)和现象学(epistemology)理论之上。中国哲学的另一个特征是反映了自然和自我，因而产生了天人合一、人在天地之间的位置，以及对差异(differentiation)和变化的阐释。

Chinese Philosophy Vocabulary in English Translation
中国哲学相关词汇与表达方式

儒家	Confucianism
孔子	Confucius
孟子	Mencius
《论语》	The Analects
《大学》	The Great Learning
《中庸》	The Doctrine of Golden Mean
仁义礼智信	benevolence, righteousness, propriety, wisdom, fidelity
罢黜百家，独尊儒术	Suppressing the Hundred Schools and Setting Confucianism as the only State Ideology
道家	Taoism

Unit 2

Philosophy

道	Dao/Tao/the Way
《易经》	*I Ching*
阴阳	Yin and Yang (the interconnection between male and female, light and dark, high and low, hot and cold, water and fire, life and death, etc.)
八卦	Bagua/eight trigrams
天人合一	harmony between man and nature
儒道互补	complementation between Confucianism and Taoism
法家	Legalism
墨家	Mohism
兼爱	fraternity/impartial caring/universal love
非攻	against warfare/renouncement of violence

Key to Unit 2 Exercises

Before You Start

1. What do you know about Chinese philosophies and philosophers? Give some names and terms for example.

Sample answer:

The most important Chinese philosophies are Confucianism and Taoism. The former was founded by Confucius in the Spring and Autumn Period, some 2,500 years ago. Confucius was not only a philosopher but a great scholar and teacher. He had many followers, among whom Mencius and Xunzi were most famous. Confucius's disciples recorded his words to make a book entitled *Lunyu*. Confucius taught us that Li (礼) and Ren(仁) should be observed in a society. A man should be kind and fulfill his duties to his family, community and state. His thought and ideas were widely discussed, refined and reinforced in ancient China and thus became the spiritual pillar of ancient Chinese government and society.

Beside Confucianism, Taoism is another equally important philosophy native to China. Taoist philosophy, also called Lao Zhuang Philosophy, had two essential figures to represent, namely, Laozi(or Lao Tzu) and Zhuangzi. Laozi was said to be the author of *Dao De Jing*, the book stating Taoist thought in about 5,000 characters. In this book Laozi tried to persuade people to follow the rules of nature. Zhuangzi, another representative of Taoism, wrote many essays and fables to support Laozi's thought as well as develop his own ideas on how things go in this world. Although Confucianism was established as the goverment thought, Taoism never ceased to exist in traditional Chinese culture.

Apart from Confucianism and Taoism, there are some other schools of philosophies in China. Mozi and his Mohism, Hanfeizi and his Legalism, and many others contributed to

Chinese philosophy.

2. Do you still remember some famous quotes from Confucius or Lao Tzu? Recite three pieces in Chinese.

Samples：

子曰：学而时习之,不亦说乎？有朋自远方来,不亦乐乎？人不知而不愠,不亦君子乎？三人行,必有我师焉。择其善者而从之,其不善者而改之。性相近也,习相远也。知之为知之,不知为不知,是知也。敏而好学,不耻下问。君子坦荡荡,小人长戚戚。

老子《道德经》名言："道可道,非常道。名可名,非常名。""人法地,地法天,天法道,道法自然。""大方无隅；大器晚成；大音希声；大象无形；道隐无名。""民不畏死,奈何以死惧之？""信言不美,美言不信。"

3. Do you believe in fortune-telling? How many ways do you know that can tell one's fortune? What are they?

Common methods used for fortune telling in Europe and the Americas include astromancy, horary astrology, pendulum reading, spirit board reading, tasseography (reading tea leaves in a cup), cartomancy (fortune telling with cards), tarot reading, crystallomancy (reading of a crystal sphere), and chiromancy (palmistry, reading of the palms). The last three have traditional associations in the popular mind with the Roma and Sinti people (often called "gypsies"). Another form of fortune-telling, sometimes called "reading" or "spiritual consultation", does not rely on specific devices or methods, but rather the practitioner gives the client advice and predictions which are said to have come from spirits or in visions. Here is a list of fortune-telling methods：

* Alectromancy：by observation of a rooster pecking at grain
* Astrology：by the movements of celestial bodies.
* Astromancy：by the stars.
* Augury：by the flight of birds.
* Bazi or four pillars：by hour, day, month, and year of birth.
* Bibliomancy：by books; frequently, but not always, religious texts.
* Cartomancy：by playing cards, tarot cards, or oracle cards.
* Ceromancy：by patterns in melting or dripping wax.
* Cheiromancy：by the shape of the hands and lines in the palms.
* Chronomancy：by determination of lucky and unlucky days.
* Clairvoyance：by spiritual vision or inner sight.
* Cleromancy：by casting of lots, or casting bones or stones.
* Cold reading：by using visual and aural clues.
* Crystallomancy：by crystal ball, also called scrying.
* Extispicy：by the entrails of animals.

* Face Reading: by means of variations in face and head shape.
* Feng shui: by earthen harmony.
* Gastromancy: by stomach-based ventriloquism (historically).
* Geomancy: by markings in the ground, sand, earth, or soil.
* Haruspicy: by the livers of sacrificed animals.
* Horary astrology: the astrology of the time the question was asked.
* Hydromancy: by water.
* *I Ching* divination: by yarrow stalks or coins and the *I Ching*.
* Kau cim(抽签): by means of numbered bamboo sticks shaken from a tube.
* Lithomancy: by stones or gems.
* Necromancy: by the dead, or by spirits or souls of the dead.
* Numerology: by numbers.
* Oneiromancy: by dreams.
* Onomancy: by names.
* Palmistry: by lines and mounds on the hand.
* Paper fortune teller: origami used in fortune-telling games
* Pendulum reading: by the movements of a suspended object.
* Pyromancy: by gazing into fire.
* Rhabdomancy: divination by rods.
* Runecasting or Runic divination: by runes.
* Scrying: by looking at or into reflective objects.
* Spirit board: by planchette or talking board.
* Taromancy: by a form of cartomancy using tarot cards.
* Tasseography or tasseomancy: by tea leaves or coffee grounds.

(Based on http://en.wikipedia.org/wiki/Fortune-telling)

Section A Reading and Writing

Exercises

1. Skimming and Scanning

(1) Y   (2) N   (3) Y   (4) Y   (5) N   (6) NG   (7) N

(8) the *Analects*

(9) meaning of existence

(10) spiritual guides

2. Translating

(1) 子曰:"学而时习之,不亦说乎? 有朋自远方来,不亦乐乎? 人不知而不愠,不亦君子乎？"

(2) 子曰："温故而知新，可以为师矣。"

(3) 子曰："人无远虑，必有近忧。"

(4) 子曰："学而不思则罔，思而不学则殆。"

(5) 孔子云："吾十有五而志于学，三十而立，四十而不惑，五十而知天命，六十而耳顺，七十而从心所欲，不逾矩。"

3. Discussing and Writing

Sample Writing

Zhuangzi was a great thinker who often stated his ideas through intriguing stories and fables, which in some way both enlighten and confuse his readers. To clarify Zhuangzi's thought through the tales he told is not easy, but not impossible. If we accept that Zhuangzi's primary point is about the limitations of individual perspectives, it would follow that he is committed to the appreciation of different perspectives.

The fable of Xiao Yao You, or "Travel in Boundless Freedom" compares two perspectives, namely, the great Kun Peng's boundless travel versus the limited vision of those small creatures: the cicada, the young dove and the quail. There is no prejudice against such small creatures. Zhuangzi only intended to make clear the distinction between the great and the small.

People may wonder how Zhuangzi achieved his disinterested understanding of the world, so the fable "Zhuang Zhou or a Butterfly" can account for his way of looking at the self and the world. In his dream Zhuangzi was a butterfly happy with himself; when he awoke, he was still pondering whether he should be Zhuang Zhou or a butterfly. If a man doesn't distinguish between a butterfly and himself, confusing dreams with reality, what difference will he make in this world?

However, Zhuangzi was not a nihilist（虚无主义者）; rather he was confident with his own feelings and judgments. His famous argument with Huizi about the happiness of fish is a good example. While Huizi questioned him against his perception of the fish's happiness, he contended that since Huizi had heard his comment about the fish, Huizi could not deny the truth that Zhuangzi knew the fish was happy. This seemingly tongue-twisting argument shows Zhuangzi's assurance of what he felt: "There is no denying that what I know is knowing."

Many of such examples in the *Zhuangzi* draw on the diversity and plurality of experiences and perspectives. The juxtaposition of human against nonhuman seems playful yet profound; these comparisons are particularly effective in demonstrating the limitations of the human perspective. Apprehending many perspectives broadens and enriches one's understanding of the world. This in turn engenders an attitude of openness in negotiation. In this case, Zhuangzi's philosophy can have broader implications for approaching discussions in a globalized context with its multiple value systems. (376 words)

Unit 2 Philosophy

Section B Listening and Speaking

Task 1 **Listening and Speaking**

(1) What is the English translation of 《易经》 other than the *I Ching*?

The *Book of Changes*.

(2) What instruments can be used for fortune-telling by the *I Ching*?

In ancient times, people divided grass sticks to have their fortune told; nowadays people toss coins to predict their fortune.

(3) Why is the *I Ching* so fascinating?

The charm of the *I Ching* lies in the very fact that things are always changing, so is one's fortune.

(4) What is the philosophical significance of the *I Ching*?

Philosophically, it is a book written to reveal the patterns (the Dao) of things changing between the heavens and earth, which in ancient Chinese refer to the world as a whole.

(5) Who wrote the *I Ching*?

Four holy men are cited as the authors of the *I Ching*, namely, Fu-xi, King Wên of Chou, the Duke of Chou, and Confucius.

Task 2 **Listening and Blank Filling**

	School of thought	Representative	Masterpiece
(1)	Confucianism	Confucius	*The Analects*
		Mencius	*Mencius*
(2)	Taoism	Lao Tzu	*Tao Te Ching*
		Zhuang Zi	*Zhuangzi*
(3)	Mohism	Mo Di	*Mozi*
(4)	Legalism	Han Fei	*Hanfeizi*
(5)	School of Names or Logicians	Gongsun Long	*Gongsun Longzi*
(6)	School of Yin-Yang	Zou Yan	*Zouzi*
(7)	The School of Diplomacy	Zhang Yi, Su Qin	
(8)	The Miscellaneous School	Lü Buwei	*Lüshi Chunqiu*

Task 3　Making a Short Speech
Sample Omitted

参考译文

　　(1) Confucius (551—479 BC) was the founder of Confucianism. He advocated（倡导）a set of moral code on the basis of five merits: benevolence（仁）, righteousness（义）, propriety（礼）, wisdom（智）and fidelity（信）. Among them, benevolence was considered as the cornerstone（基石）of his philosophy, which stands for faithfulness, filial piety（孝道）, tolerance and kindness. He also requested people to keep in good harmony with each other and establish a community ruled by standard manners and behavior. One of his followers, Mencius (372—289BC), repeatedly tried to convince rulers that the ruler should cultivate（培养）moral perfection in order to set a good example to the people and the ruler who governed benevolently would earn the respect of the people.

　　(2) Chinese philosophy has a history of several thousand years; its origins are often traced back to the *I Ching* (the *Book of Changes*), which introduced some of the most fundamental（基本的）terms of Chinese philosophy. The central focus of Chinese philosophy throughout the ages has been a practical concern with man and society, how to live an ideal life, and how best to organize society. Ethics（伦理）and political philosophy have often taken precedence over metaphysics（形而上学）and epistemology（认识论）. Another characteristic of Chinese philosophy has been reflections on nature and the self, which has resulted in the development of themes like the unity between man and Heaven, the place of man in the cosmic（宇宙的）order, and the explanations of differentiation（差异）and change.

Unit 3

Language and Literature

导读

本单元旨在通过对中国古典文学作品的简要介绍,让学生在理解的基础上学会相关的语言知识,加深对中华文学精髓的理解,并能够运用所学的相关知识和语言技能,在对外交流过程中更好的宣扬本民族的文学与文化。

Before You Start

While you are preparing for this unit, think about the following questions:
1. Have you read the novel *Romance of the Three Kingdoms* before? In your opinion, what makes it a classic novel?
2. Who is your favorite poet of the Tang Dynasty? What are the features of his works?

Section A Reading and Writing

Text 1 Romance of the Three Kingdoms

①*Romance of the Three Kingdoms*, written by Luo Guanzhong in the Ming Dynasty, is a historical novel set during the turbulent years near the end of the Han Dynasty and the Three Kingdoms era of Chinese history, starting in 169 A.D. and ending with the reunification of the land in 280 A.D.

The great novel records the period when dozens of feudal (封建的) warlords (军阀) tried to replace the declining Han Dynasty or restore it. After many years of wars, three powerful political groups remained, which eventually formed the three states of Wei, Shu, and Wu. ②It also gives readers a sense of how the Chinese view their history in a cyclical lens. The famous opening lines of the novel summarize this view: "It is a general truth of this world that anything long divided will surely unite, and anything long united will surely

divide"(话说天下大势,分久必合,合久必分).

Romance of the Three Kingdoms is regarded as one of the "Four Great Classical Novels" of Chinese literature. ③The novel is among the most beloved works of literature in East Asia, and its literary influence in the region has been compared to that of the works of Shakespeare on English literature. The charm of the novel lasts for centuries and it is still one of the most widely-read classical literary works in modern China.

Romance of the Three Kingdoms is characterized by the extreme complexity of its plot structure and hundreds of vividly-depicted characters in it. The novel consists of one hundred and twenty chapters and contains numerous secondary stories. Dominant themes of the novel include: the rise of the ideal feudal lord(主公)(Liu Bei) who finds the ideal minister(大臣)(Zhuge Liang); the conflict between the ideal lord(Liu Bei) and his biggest enemy(Cao Cao); and the cruelties of war, injustice of feudal government and ruthless struggles among different political groups.

Just as mentioned previously, some critics have argued that the opening statement—"It is a general truth of this world that anything long divided will surely unite, and anything long united will surely divide"—reflects the main theme of the novel. However, this interpretation of the novel has been refuted by others. Though the work shows the journey from unity to division in the final years of the Han Dynasty, that is only the beginning of the book. ④The author expended most of his ink on the focal point of his description—the difficult transition from "division" to "unity" and the great achievements that came out of the bitter struggles by various heroes to reunify the Chinese empire. (461 words)

(Adapted from: http://en.wikipedia.org/wiki/Romance_of_the_Three_Kingdoms)

Difficult Sentences

① *Romance of the Three Kingdoms*, written by Luo Guanzhong in the Ming Dynasty, is a historical novel set during the turbulent years near the end of the Han Dynasty and the Three Kingdoms era of Chinese history, starting in 169 A.D. and ending with the reunification of the land in 280 A.D.
由明代小说家罗贯中创作的历史小说《三国演义》以中国汉朝末年的乱世和三国时期为时代背景,从公元169年开始,至公元280年三国统一结束。

② It also gives readers a sense of how the Chinese view their history in a cyclical lens.
本书也使读者了解到中国人是如何以一种循环反复的视角来看待他们的历史的。

③ The novel is among the most beloved works of literature in East Asia, and its literary influence in the region has been compared to that of the works of Shakespeare on English literature.

这部小说是东亚地区最受欢迎的文学作品之一,它对东亚文学的影响等同于莎士比亚对英国文学的影响。

④ The author expended most of his ink on the focal point of his description—the difficult transition from "division" to "unity" and the great achievements that came out of the bitter struggles by various heroes to reunify the Chinese empire.

作者运用大量的笔墨重点描绘了从"分裂"到"统一"的艰难转变以及各种英雄人物在统一中国的艰苦奋斗中取得的丰功伟绩。

Text 2 Poetry of the Tang Dynasty

The Tang Dynasty is the heyday (鼎盛时期) of imperial China, politically, economically and culturally. One great literary achievement of that period is poetry. Tang poetry is not only one of the excellent literature heritages of China, but also regarded as a bright pearl of literature treasure of the world. Hundreds of famous poets at that time are remembered by future generations, including great masters like Li Bai, Du Fu and Bai Juyi. Besides them, there are a lot more—over 2,300 poets still have their names heard until today. More than 48,900 pieces of poems have been compiled in the *Complete Poetry of Tang*(《全唐诗》).

Poetry during that period contains a wide range of themes. ①Some reflect the social situations and conflicts at that time from side and reveal the darkness of feudal society; some sing the praises of just wars and express patriotic thought; some depict the beauty of the homeland; in addition, some describe personal aspirations and encounters, affection, friendship as well as joys and sorrows of life. Some of those poems are realistic and some others romantic while many great works are the models of the combination of realism and romanticism.

Besides themes, the form of Tang poetry is also diversified. ② The verse is divided into two categories: four-lined and eight-lined, both of which can be further divided into five-character and seven-character ones. Therefore, the basic forms of Tang poetry are five-character four-lined poems, seven-character four-lined poems, five-character eight-lined poems and seven-character eight-lined poems. The verse has strong restriction on phonology (音律) and form.

The form and style of Tang poetry are colorful and creative, not only inheriting the tradition of folk songs in Han, Wei Yuefu① (乐府), but also developing the pattern of song form greatly; ③not only inheriting the five-character and seven-character ancient verse of the former dynasties, but also developing them into the long poem for narration and sentimental stories by extending the usage of five-character and seven-character forms, which is especially elegant and regular in style. ④The creation and maturation of the Tang poetry pushes the artistic features of harmonious syllable and refined words of ancient verse up to an unprecedented level and helps the ancient lyric to find a most typical form, which is still favored by people today. (406 words)

(Adapted from: http://www.teachcn.com/Content.asp? id=1045)

Difficult Sentences

① Some reflect the social situations and conflicts at that time from side and reveal the darkness of feudal society; some sing the praises of just wars and express patriotic thought; some depict the beauty of the homeland; in addition, some describe personal aspirations and encounters, affection, friendship as well as joys and sorrows of life
有些诗歌从侧面反映了当时社会状况和矛盾,揭示了封建社会的黑暗;有些诗歌则歌颂正义的战争,抒发爱国主义情怀;有些诗歌描述了故乡的美景;也有的诗歌表现个人抱负、际遇、爱情、友情以及生活中的喜怒哀乐。

② The verse is divided into two categories: four-lined and eight-lined, both of which can be further divided into five-character and seven-character ones.
这些诗歌分为两类:绝句和律诗;绝句和律诗又分别分为五言和七言。

③ ... not only inheriting the five-character and seven-character ancient verse of the former dynasties, but also developing them into the long poem for narration and sentimental stories by extending the usage of five-character and seven-character forms, which is especially elegant and regular in style.
(这些诗歌)不仅继承了前朝诗歌的五言和七言的形式,并且借用这种形式,发展出了叙事和抒情的长诗。这种长诗在形式上非常优雅和规整。

④ The creation and maturation of the Tang poetry pushes the artistic features of harmonious syllable and refined words of ancient verse up to an unprecedented level and helps the ancient lyric to find a most typical form, which is still favored by people today.
唐诗的产生和成熟使得古诗的韵律和谐、辞藻华丽这一艺术特点达到了顶峰,并且为古诗提供了一种别具特色的表现形式,这种形式时至今日仍为人所推崇。

---

① 乐府是自秦代以来设立的配置乐曲、训练乐工和采集民歌的专门官署,汉乐府指由汉时乐府机关所采制的诗歌。这些诗,原本在民间流传,经由乐府保存下来,汉人叫做"歌诗",魏晋时始称"乐府"或"汉乐府"。后世文人仿此形式所作的诗,亦称"乐府诗"。

Unit 3
Language and Literature

Exercises

Task 1   Reading Comprehension

Directions: *Decide whether the following statements are TRUE or FALSE according to the two passages you have read.*

(　　) (1) *Romance of the Three Kingdoms* is highly regarded in the history of Chinese literature.

(　　) (2) The novel is famous for its complex plot structure as well as the extreme difficulty in understanding it.

(　　) (3) The novel reflects the inhumanity（残酷）of war and social injustice of feudal China.

(　　) (4) Tang poetry covers a wide range of themes and subjects and has various artistic styles.

(　　) (5) In spite of the prosperity of Tang poetry in ancient days, only a limited number of poems are available today.

Task 2   Vocabulary Building

Directions: *Complete the following sentences with the words listed below. Change the forms if necessary.*

| decline | restore | vivid | dominant | refute |
| aspiration | compile | patriotic | category | unprecedented |

(1) We have spent much time in _____ a list of suitable people for the job.

(2) Ageing is the _____ of energy and vigor with the passing of time.

(3) The novel presents a _____ picture of life in the center of Africa.

(4) The newly elected government is taking a series of measures to _____ order after the civil war（内战）.

(5) Peace and development are the _____ themes of the modern age.

(6) Professor Smith _____ the idea put forward by Dr. Johnson in the conference.

(7) The _____ of becoming the President of the United States was frustrated by a number of failures.

(8) The movie received _____ success, as a result of the hard work of the director, the actors as well as other members of the team.

(9) They misplaced that book under another _____.

(10) Strong _____ sentiment was aroused by the works of that poet.

47

Task 3 Translating

Directions: *Translate the following English poems back into Chinese.*

> **Spring Morning**
>
> This morning of spring in bed I'm lying,
> Not to awake till birds are crying.
> After one night of wind and showers,
> How many are the fallen flowers?

> **Snow on the River**
>
> From hills to hills no bird in flight
> From paths to paths no man in sight.
> A lonely fisherman afloat,
> Is fishing snow in a lonely boat.

> **Returning Home**
>
> Young, I left home and not till old do I come back,
> Unchanged is my accent, yet my hair no longer black.
> The children whom I meet on the way don't know me,
> "Where are you from, sir?" they smile and ask with glee.

Task 4 Discussing and Writing

Directions: *Who is the most impressive character in* Romance of the Three Kingdoms? *What are the characteristics that impress you most? Discuss this topic in class with your classmates and then write an essay introducing this character. You should write at least 200 words telling us who he/she is, what he/she has done and why this person impresses you.*

Section B Listening and Speaking

Text 3 Situational Dialogue: About *Journey to the West*

(H: Howard, an American student learning Chinese in China; L: Li Ping, a Chinese student.)

H: The TV series *Journey to the West* seems very popular in China. It's on TV during nearly every summer vacation.

L: Yes. We have been watching it again and again since childhood.

H: Wow! It is adapted from a very classical novel, isn't it?

L: Yes. *Journey to the West*. One of the "Four Great Classical Novels of Chinese Literature".

H: OK. Would you please tell me something about that novel?

L: It was completed at the mid-Ming Dynasty by Wu Cheng'en, a writer born in the south of China (now Jiangsu Province). The novel mainly depicts the story of Monk Tang and his disciples (徒弟) going west to seek for sutra (佛经).

H: There are lots of exciting stories in the book, aren't there?

L: Yes. On the way to India, where the Buddha (佛祖) lives, there are countless monsters, demons and evil spirits (妖魔鬼怪). So Monk Tang has three disciples for protection.

H: The Monkey King is one of them and he is the most powerful and skillful one.

L: You are right. ①He is rebellious, mischievous and cute. He once fights against the Heaven Court of the Jade Emperor(玉帝) and almost wins the war. Unfortunately, he ends up being under a great mountain for 500 years. ②After becoming a disciple of Monk Tang, he goes through a whole lot of obstacles so that finally with his protection Monk Tang brings back the True Sutra.

H: He is such a great hero! Is he the favorite character of yours?

L: Of course he is. Not only mine, but also most Chinese readers'. ③He symbolizes heroism and courage in the mind of Chinese people.

H: I want to read the book, but I'm afraid I cannot understand the words in it.

L: You can start by watching the TV series. But the original book is much greater than what is on TV. Besides the wonderful stories, the book also reflects the social reality of the Ming Dynasty and criticizes the existing ugliness of the society. It enjoys a very important position in the history of Chinese literature

H: I'll learn Chinese very hard and one day I'll read the book by myself.

L: I'm sure you will.

Difficult Sentences

① He is rebellious, mischievous and cute.
   他很叛逆、调皮,但也很可爱。

② After becoming a disciple of Monk Tang, he went through a whole lot of obstacles so

that finally with his protection Monk Tang brought back the True Sutra.
在成为唐僧的徒弟后,他历经种种磨难;而最终在他的保护下,唐僧取回了真经。

③ He symbolizes heroism and courage in the mind of Chinese people.
在中国人心里他是英雄主义和勇气的象征。

Text 4 Lecture: An Introduction to Traditional Chinese Literature in Part

China is the only country in the world with a literature written in one language for more than 3,000 consecutive years. Traditional Chinese literature mostly consists of works written in classical Chinese (文言文). For more than one thousand years, this form of literature has been the subject matter of the Imperial Examinations (科举考试), but inaccessible to people of the lower class.

The traditional Chinese literature concerns itself with the serious questions of poetry, philosophy and history. The *I Ching* or *Yijing* (《易经》) is possibly the most influential book of Chinese philosophy. It is essentially a book of divination (占卜). ① Via a series of hexagrams (卦), the elaborate ritual of divination enables the reader to obtain a "judgment", which is generally rather vague and demands a huge amount of subjective interpretation. Nevertheless, the *I Ching* has been studied by almost every influential Chinese thinker, including Lao Tzu (Lao Zi), who based some of his Taoist theory on it. Other classical writings related to Taoism are *Tao Te Ching* or *Dao De Jing* (《道德经》), written by Lao Tzu himself and *Chuang Tzu* or *Zhuang Zi* (《庄子》), a collection of parables by Chuang Tzu (Zhuang Zi), who is the second great sage (圣人) of Taoism.

The most important work of the Confucian literary heritage is the *Analects* (《论语》). Compiled by Confucius' disciples, it records the master's activities and conversations. Since the time when Confucianism became widely accepted, ② the laconic and provocative sentences of this work have exercised a profound impact upon the thought and language of Chinese intellectuals. For the last hundreds of years, it has become a basic textbook in the schools.

Poetry also has a long history and is an indispensable part of traditional literature of China. The oldest poems were compiled in the *Book of Songs* (《诗经》), which was composed during the Western Zhou Dynasty (西周, 1100 B.C.—770 B.C.) and the Spring and Autumn Period (春秋时期, 770 B.C.—476 B.C.). Edited by Confucius, it is an anthology of about three hundred poems. Some of them are folk songs from the feudal states of early Zhou while others are songs used by the nobles in sacrificial ceremonies (祭祀) or at banquets. Poetry reached a zenith (顶峰) in Tang Dynasty (618 A.D.—907 A.D.). The most famous poets during this time are Li Bai and Du Fu. Li was the greatest romantic poet in ancient China. ③ His poems, permeated with romanticism, are vigorous, enthusiastic and lucid. His anthology (选集) contains about 1,000 poems, ④ covering a wide range of subjects from the exposure of corruption of the court and the hard life and suffering of the common people, to the description of magnificent scenery of the country as well as the praise of true friendship and the expression of his ideals and feelings. As Li Bai's contemporary, Du is often viewed as the greatest poet of realism in ancient China. As a mirror of his time, his poems faithfully and profoundly reflect the social realities of the country in decline. In 759, Du gave up his official post and went to Sichuan Province, living in a thatched hut (草屋) on the outskirts of Chengdu. More than 1,400 of his poems are retained to the present-day, covering various aspects of the society of his time. ⑤ Many of them are penetrating exposures of the cruelty of the ruling class and the suffering of the people. (608 *words*)

(Based on http://www.topchinatravel.com/china-guide/chinese-classical-literature)

Difficult Sentences

① Via a series of hexagrams, the elaborate ritual of divination enables the reader to obtain a "judgment", which is generally rather vague and demands a huge amount of subjective interpretation.
占卜的复杂仪式通过一系列的卦让求卦者获得一个"判断",但这个判断通常是模棱两可的,并且需要大量的主观的阐释。

② the laconic and provocative sentences of this work have exercised a profound impact upon the thought and language of Chinese intellectuals.
《论语》简明而又发人深省的语言对中国的知识分子的思想和语言产生了深刻的影响。

③ His poems, permeated with romanticism, are vigorous, enthusiastic and lucid.
他的诗歌充满了浪漫主义情怀、强劲有力、激情洋溢而又清晰易懂。

④ covering a wide range of subjects from the exposition of corruption of the court and the hard life and suffering of the common people, to the description of magnificent scenery of the country as well as the praise of true friendship and the expression of his ideals and feelings.
他的诗歌题材广泛,有的揭示了宫廷生活的腐败和老百姓生活的艰辛,有的描绘了祖国的壮丽景色,有的歌颂了诚挚的友谊,有的则抒发了他自己的理想与情怀。

⑤ Many of them are penetrating exposures of the cruelty of the ruling class and the sufferings of the people.
许多作品都犀利地揭示了统治阶级的残酷以及老百姓的苦难。

Exercises

Task 1 Listening and Speaking

Directions: *Listen to the dialogue twice and summarize the main plot of* Journey to the West. *Then introduce it to foreign friends in your own language.*

Task 2 Listening Comprehension

Directions: *Listen to the lecture on Traditional Chinese Literature in Part twice and take some notes, then complete the following statements by choosing the proper answer from A, B, C and D.*

(1) China has a literature written in one language for more than _____ consecutive years.

　　A. 1,000　　　　B. 3,000　　　　C. 5,000　　　　D. 10,000

(2) _____ is possibly the most influential book of Chinese philosophy.

　　A. *I Ching/Yi Jing*(《易经》)

　　B. *Romance of the Three Kingdoms*

　　C. *Tao Te Ching/Dao De Jing*(《道德经》)

　　D. *Book of Songs*(《诗经》)

(3) Lao Tzu and _____ are the two great sages of Taosim.

　　A. Confucius　　　　　　　　B. Mencius

　　C. Sun Tzu　　　　　　　　　D. Chuang Tzu/Zhuang Zi

(4) The oldest poems were compiled in _____, which was composed during the Western Zhou Dynasty

　　A. *Book of Songs*(《诗经》)　　　B. *Complete Poetry of Tang*

　　C. *I Ching/Yi Jing*(《易经》)　　　D. *Li Sao/The Lament*(《离骚》)

(5) The most famous poets during Tang Dynasty are Li Bai and Du Fu. Li is the greatest _____ poet in ancient China.

　　A. realistic　　　B. pessimistic　　　C. romantic　　　D. modernistic

Task 3 Vocabulary Building

Directions: *Complete the following sentences with the words listed below. Change the forms if necessary.*

inaccessible	elaborate	heritage	profound	consist
intellectual	ceremony	enthusiasm	contemporary	vigorous

(1) There will be a/an _____ next week honoring the veteran soldiers of the country.

(2) His _____ breathed new life to the company and moved every employee.

(3) A child should learn as much as possible in this crucial phase of _____ development.

(4) After the new library is completed, every citizen will have free _____ to many good books and other learning resources.

(5) Everyone in the class was impressed by the _____ knowledge of the professor.

(6) Can you _____ on that event? There are many details unknown to us.

(7) A novelist must be able to make use of the cultural _____ of his/her native country.

(8) Though an expert on classical Roman and Greek literature, Dr. Johnson knows little about _____ literary works of Europe.

(9) How many players does a rugby team _____ of?

(10) Old as Jamie is, he is nonetheless _____ and active.

Task 4 Translating

Directions: *Translate the following Chinese sentences into English by using expressions from the texts.*

(1) 这部电影是由史蒂芬·金(Stephen King)的一部畅销小说改编的。(adapt)
_____

(2) 在经历了许多磨难以后，他最终获得了成功。(a whole lot of obstacles)
_____

(3) 孔子的思想对中国社会与文化产生了深远的影响。(exercise a profound impact)
_____

(4) 杜甫的诗歌揭露了中国封建社会的腐败和黑暗。(expose; corruption)
_____

(5) 小说的最后一章是全书不可分割的一部分。(chapter; indispensable)
_____

Translation Practice

Directions: *Translate the following passages into English.*

(1) "送别"是唐诗里常见的主题。通过赠诗给一个即将离别的友人，诗人常常表达自己的悲伤之情。送别诗里常用的意象(image)有音乐、酒和柳枝。音乐是送别仪式必不可少的部分。音乐通常由琵琶等古典乐器演奏，旋律优美而悲伤。在这种场合，喝酒也是必要的。也许这是因为酒能够让人得到安慰，忘却生活中的烦恼以及与友人离别的愁绪。送别的另一个风俗便是为友人送上柳枝。因为"柳"和"留"同音。通过这种方式，诗人就表达了让友人永远留下来的愿望。

(2)《红楼梦》(*Dream of the Red Mansions*)是中国文学"四大名著"之一。它写于18世纪中叶，并被认为是中国文学中的杰作(masterpiece)以及中国小说史上的顶峰。许多学者都致力于该作品的研究，而这个研究领域也被称作"红学"(Redology)。人们通常认为该小说反映了作者曹雪芹自己的经历以及他家族的兴衰。该书的优秀之处不仅在于它的情节和人物塑造(characterization)，同时也在于它对当时社会生活结构的精确、细节的描写。几个世纪以来，小说中的许多词句已经融入了中国人的日常语言。由此可见该书经久不衰的魅力。

Words and Expressions Related to Traditional Chinese Literature
中国古典文学相关词汇与表达方式

Chinese classical literature	中国古典文学	Literary Chinese, or Classical Chinese	文言文
Shi Jing, or *The Classic of Poetry*, or *The Book of Songs*	《诗经》	poetry/poem	诗
Chu Ci, or *Verses of Chu*	《楚辞》	verse/stanza	（诗）节
Li Sao, or *The Lament*	《离骚》	rhyme	韵
Mulan Ci, or *The Ballad of Mulan*	《木兰辞》	line	（诗）行
The Peafowl Flying Southeast, or *The Ballad of a Tragic Couple*	《孔雀东南飞》	Yuefu Poetry	乐府诗
Tao Hua Yuan Ji, or *The Peach Blossom Spring*	《桃花源记》	*Wen Xin Diao Long*, or *The Literary Mind and the Carving of Dragons*	《文心雕龙》
Xi Xiang Ji, or *Romance of the Western Chamber*	《西厢记》	*Ci*, or Songci poetry	（宋）词
Shui Hu Zhuan, or *Water Margin*, or *Outlaws of the Marsh*	《水浒传》	Zaju Drama of Yuan Dynasty	元杂剧
Dream of Red Mansions	《红楼梦》	*Dou E Yuan*, or *The Injustice to Dou E*, also known as *Snow in Midsummer*	《窦娥冤》

Key to Unit 3 Exercises

Before You Start

1. *Romance of the Three Kingdoms* is a 120-chapter historical novel with its subject drawing from the history between the last years of the Eastern Han Dynasty and the Three Kingdoms Period. Special emphasis is laid on Liu Bei and Cao Cao, two antagonistic figures in the ruling class. Liu was portrayed as an ideal ruler, while Cao was a famous statesman and strategist. Taking the conflicts and struggles as a major clue and wars as plots, the writer stringed hundreds of tales together with distinct cause and effect, and combined facts with imagination, details with sketches, creating a masterpiece that is surpassed by few in Chinese history.

2. My favorite poet of Tang Dynasty is Bai Juyi. His artistic style is different from those of his contemporaries'. Bai led a group of poets who rejected the courtly style of the time and emphasized the didactic function of literature, believing that every literary work should contain a fitting moral and a well-defined social purpose. His most important contributions to poetry are his satirical and allegorical ballads and his "new Yuefu," which usually took the form of free verse based on old folk ballads. The most prolific of the Tang

poets, Bai aimed for simplicity in his writing, and he was deeply concerned with the social problems of the time; he deplored the dissolute and decadent lifestyles of corrupt officials and sympathized with the sufferings of the poor.

Section A Reading and Writing

Task 1   **Reading Comprehension**

(1) T   (2) F   (3) T   (4) T   (5) F

Task 2   **Vocabulary Building**

(1) compiling   (2) decline   (3) vivid   (4) restore   (5) dominant

(6) refuted   (7) aspiration   (8) unprecedented   (9) category

(10) patriotic

Task 3   **Translating**

春晓 （孟浩然） 春眠不觉晓， 处处闻啼鸟。 夜来风雨声， 花落知多少。	江雪 （柳宗元） 千山鸟飞绝， 万径人踪灭。 孤舟蓑笠翁， 独钓寒江雪。	回乡偶书 （贺知章） 少小离家老大回， 乡音无改鬓毛衰。 儿童相见不相识， 笑问客从何处来。

Task 4   **Discussing and Writing**

Sample Writing

Among hundreds of vividly depicted characters in *Romance of the Three Kingdoms*, the most impressive one to me is Liu Bei, the founder of the State Shu. Though the novel describes him as a kind, merciful lord, he is in fact hypocritical. The mercifulness he shows is nothing but the tool he uses to control other people.

One event is often mentioned to illustrate how kind he is and how much he cares about people working for him. However, we can easily find how hypocritical he is if we take a close look at it.

During a battle against Cao Cao, he angrily throws away his baby son Liu Chan when General Zhao Yun risks his own life to rescue the baby and take him back. Seeing what Liu has done, General Zhao is so touched and swears in a crying tone that he will defend the Liu family to his death. But as a matter of fact, Liu does care about his own son, which is what a normal father should do. If he really valued General Zhao more than his own baby and were angry about the baby, he could have killed him or thrown him away from a mountain top instead of throwing him onto the soft mud ground, which does no harm to the baby at all. But his acting is so vivid that General Zhao is convinced that Liu is a great lord. (238 *words*)

Section B Listening and Speaking

Task 1 **Listening and Speaking**

Sample Answer:

Journey to the West is one of the "Four Great Classical Novels of Chinese Literature". It was completed at the mid-Ming Dynasty by Wu Cheng'en, from Jiangsu Province. The novel is mainly about the story of Monk Tang and his three disciples going west to seek for sutra. On the way to India, where the Buddha lives, there are countless monsters, demons and evil spirits who attempt to eat Monk Tang. But under the protection of his disciples—Monkey King, General Pig and Monk Sha, Monk Tang finally arrives in India and takes back the sutra. Monkey King is the main character of the novel. He is rebellious and mischievous. On the other hand, he is powerful and brave, symbolizing heroism and courage. (122 *words*)

Task 2 **Listening Comprehension**

(1) B (2) A (3) D (4) A (5) C

Task 3 **Vocabulary Building**

(1) ceremony (2) enthusiasm (3) intellectual (4) access

(5) profound (6) elaborate (7) heritage (8) contemporary

(9) consist (10) vigorous

Task 4 **Translating**

(1) The movie is adapted from a best-seller by Stephen King.

(2) Having gone through a whole lot of obstacles, he finally succeeded.

(3) The thoughts of Confucius have exercised a profound impact on Chinese society and culture.

(4) Du Fu's poems exposed the corruption and darkness of the society of feudal China.

(5) The last chapter of the novel is an indispensable part of the whole book.

参考译文

(1) "Parting" was a common theme in Tang poetry. By writing a poem to a friend who was leaving, the poet usually showed his sorrow and sadness. Images frequently used in a parting poem included music, liquor and a willow twig. Music was an important section of the parting ceremony. The music, which was often melodious and sorrowful, was played by traditional instruments such as 'Pipa'. Drinking liquor was also a necessary part on these occasions. Perhaps it was because liquor could console(安慰) people and help them forget troubles in life and the sadness of parting from a friend. Another custom was giving a willow twig to the leaving friend, since 'willow' in Chinese has the same pronunciation of that of 'stay'. In this way, the poet expressed his wish that his friend stay with him forever.

(2) *Dream of the Red Mansions* is one of the Four Great Classical Novels of Chinese literature. It was written in the middle of the 18th century and considered as a masterpiece(杰作) of Chinese literature as well as the peak of Chinese fiction. Many scholars are devoted to the study of this novel and the field of study is known as 'Redology'. The novel is usually thought to be reflecting the experience of the author Cao Xueqin and the rise and decline of his own family. It is remarkable for not only its plot and characterization(角色塑造), but also its precise and detailed observation of the life and social structures of that time. For centuries, a huge number of words and expressions from the novel have already been incorporated(融入) into the daily language of Chinese people, which demonstrates the ever-lasting charm of the book.

Unit 4

Education in Ancient China

导读

本单元旨在通过对中国古代教育制度的简要介绍,使学生融会贯通相关的语言与文化知识,加深对中国古代教育理念和精髓的理解,并在对外交流中更好的宣扬本民族的文明与文化。

Before You Start

While you are preparing for this unit, think about the following questions:
1. What do you know about the ways ancient Chinese people received education?
2. What was the purpose of the Imperial Examination (科举考试) in ancient China?
3. How many famous ancient Chinese academies (书院) do you know? What are they?

Section A Reading and Writing

Text 1 History of Ancient Chinese Education

China's ancient education was one of the most splendid components of ancient Chinese culture. Chinese education has a long history dating from the Xia, Shang and Zhou dynasties 3,000/4,000 years ago.

In the Shang Dynasty (16th—11th century BC), formal schools emerged with the names like "Xiao" (school), "Xue" (study) and "Daxue" (higher school). Teachers then were all government officials and students were all children of the nobility, so that was the earliest "Guan Xue" (Government School/Education).

Education became more popular by the Spring and Autumn/Warring States Period(春秋战国时期). Confucius became the earliest founder for "Private Education". This type of private school education is often known as "Si Xue" (private institution).

Unit 4
Education in Ancient China

From Han till Qing Dynasty, the formation of government institution had been well-established. All the teaching materials and educational training were geared towards the preparation for Imperial Examination. After receiving a title in the Imperial Examination, one might receive a post in the state bureaucracy(政府机构). At the same time, private schools were also developing. Most of the famous philosophers and scientists originated from private schools.

Apart from schooling, "Family education" began to play an important role. Many of the famous historical figures grew up under the education and strict "teaching" by their parents or other senior family members, and they studied hard in order to become successful. ①For instance, it was well documented that Mencius's① mother had moved three times with her son before she eventually found a proper neighborhood for her son's education.

②After the Han dynasty, because of the increased status of Confucianism and its influence, the teaching of "poetry and rites"(诗礼) became the basic content for family education. Loyalty(忠), Filial Piety(孝), Benevolence (仁) and Righteousness (义) were core values taught in family education.

In ancient Chinese education, there was another form of education system known as "Xue Shu Jiao Yu"(学塾教育). This belongs to neither an institute education nor a family education. These are generally "primary schools for the folks". Sometimes, they were called "Meng Guan"(蒙馆)(primary education hall), "Si Shu" (private school), "Zu Xue" (族学, extended family school), etc. Most students would first learn how to read characters, then they would learn *The Three Character Classic* (《三字经》), *The Hundred Family Surnames*(《百家姓》), and *The Thousand Character Classic* (《千字文》). Then they would learn the "Four Books" (四书②). ③In addition, they would also learn Chinese calligraphy and character pairing. In this type of school, the rules and regulations were especially strict.

There were other methods such as Academies(书院), and Directorate of Education(国子监③). They all formed a unique way of knowledge teaching and became an important system for the development on "study of knowledge", "teaching method", etc. All of these formed the basis for today's Chinese education. (470 words)

(Based on http://www.chinahistoryforum.com/index.php? /topic/13449-history-of-Chinese-education/)

---

① 孟子(公元前371—前289),中国战国时期哲学家,政治家,教育家,继孔子之后儒家最重要的代表人物。
② 四书,指的是儒家四部经典:《大学》、《中庸》、《论语》、《孟子》。
③ 国子监或国子学,是中国古代封建社会国家管理教育的最高行政机关和国家设立的最高学府。明朝时期行使双京制,在南京、北京分别都设有国子监,设在南京的国子监被称为"南监",而设在北京的国子监则被称为"北监",始建于公元1306年。清末改革学制,1905年12月6日设学部,国子监裁废,其教育行政功能并入学部。

北京国子监是元、明、清三代的最高学府,也是当时朝廷掌管国学政令的最高官署。

Words and Expressions for Ancient Chinese Education
中国古代教育相关英语词汇和表达方式

the Spring and Autumn period	春秋时期
the Warring States period	战国时期
Government School/Education	官学
private institution	私学
Three Character Classic	《三字经》
Hundred Family Surnames	《百家姓》
Thousand Character Classic	《千字文》
Four Books and Five Classics	四书五经
private school	私塾
Chinese calligraphy	中国书法
character pairing	作对子

Difficult Sentences

① For instance, it was well documented that Mencius's mother had moved three times with her son before she eventually found a proper neighborhood for his education.
例如,史书上详细记载了孟子的母亲三次搬迁,最终为儿子找到了有利于学习的好环境。

② After the Han dynasty, because of the increased status of Confucianism and its influence, the teaching of "poetry and rites" became the basic content for "family education".

Unit 4
Education in Ancient China

汉代之后，由于儒学地位和影响力的加强，"诗礼之教"成为"家庭教育"的基本内容。

③ In addition, they will also learn Chinese calligraphy and character pairing.

除此之外，他们也学习中国书法和作对子。

Text 2　Confucian Educational Theory

The historical importance of education in Chinese culture is derived from the teachings of Confucius. The connection between Confucius and the official Chinese educational system thus became permanently linked right into the present time.

①Confucius broke the rule of "Xue Zai Guan Fu" (learning at the government hall, "学在官府")①. He encouraged "learning for all hierarchical levels and for all ages"("有教无类")②, and opened the door of education to the commoners. He established his own school and started to spread his teaching, thoughts and views. He became the earliest founder for "Private Education".

Confucius

In ancient Chinese education, whether they were government schools or private schools, they all placed a great emphasis on humanities and cultural education, which focused on the teaching of morality and the development of wisdom. It covered philosophy, language, literature and other cultural subjects. The curriculum at the Great Academy was based on the Confucian Five Classics(五经③).

Confucius taught his students morality, proper speech, government, and the refined arts. While he also emphasized the "Six Arts"("六艺") — ritual(礼), music(乐), archery(射), chariot-riding(御), calligraphy(书), and computation(数)— it is clear that he regarded morality as the most important subject.

Confucius is regarded as the pioneer founder of family education. According to *The Analects of Confucius*, Confucius wanted his son to learn both poetry and rites. ②He said, "If one does not learn poetry, one will not be able to talk properly", "If one does not learn rites, one will never be well footed in the society."

Other than placing a strong emphasis on morality education, Confucian education also emphasized greatly on learning/teaching method and principles. Below are some common

---

① 商周时期，官府垄断了学校教育和一切学术文化。那时，只有贵族才有机会接受教育，平民百姓不能进入校门。这种官学合一的现象，被称为"学在官府"。"学在官府"是西周教育的显著特点，也是我国奴隶社会教育制度的重要特征。

② 出自《论语·卫灵公》。类：类别。不管什么人都可以受到教育。"有教无类"的本义是不分贵族与平民，不分国界与华夷，只要有心向学，都可以入学受教。"有教无类"思想的实施，扩大了教育的社会基础和人才来源，在教育发展史上具有划时代的意义。

③ 五经，即儒家指定必读的五部典籍：《诗经》《尚书》《礼记》《易经》《春秋》。

Confucian educational philosophies:

- Revise the old in order to deduce new things. （温故知新）
- Learning and thinking are equally important. （学思并重）
- Learn in a systematic and progressive way, from a beginner's level to the advanced. （循序渐进）
- Inspiration and Guidance （启发诱导）
- Teach according to students' ability; use appropriate materials for teaching. （因材施教）

③Confucius's goal is to create gentlemen who carry themselves with grace, speak correctly, and demonstrate integrity in all things. The Master said in *The Analects* that:

"Is it not delightful to acquire knowledge and put it into practice from time to time?" ("学而时习之,不亦说乎?")①

"Learning without thought is labor lost; thought without learning is perilous." ("学而不思则罔,思而不学则殆")②

Confucius's main educational thoughts were to teach students according to their aptitude, to treat students equally and to inspire thinking. ④ His pedagogical methods were striking. He posed questions, cited passages from the classics, or used apt(恰当的) analogies(类比), and waited for his students to arrive at the right answers. He said, "I only instruct the eager and enlighten the fervent. If I hold up one corner and a student cannot come back to me with the other three, I do not go on with the lesson."

The status of education remains high in Confucian heritage cultures in East Asia. Beyond that, translations of Confucian texts influenced European thinkers of the period as well, particularly among the philosophical groups of the Enlightenment③ who were interested in the integration of the system of morality of Confucius into Western civilization. The French philosopher Voltaire④ was also influenced by Confucius, seeing the concept of Confucian rationalism as an alternative to Christian dogma. He praised Confucian ethics and politics, portraying China as a model for Europe. (568 words)

(Based on http://www.newfoundations.com/GALLERY/Confucius.html)

---

① 《论语》开篇第一句:"学而时习之,不亦说乎?""学"即取得知识,"习"即付诸实践,"说"字和"悦"字通用,意为喜悦愉快。整句的意思是:得到了知识,并且经常应用,那不是很愉快吗?

② 语出《论语·为政》——子曰:"学而不思则罔,思而不学则殆。"罔,作蒙蔽、欺骗解;殆,指危险。本句意思是:学习而不思考,人会被知识的表象所蒙蔽;思考而不学习,则会因为疑惑而更加危险。这句话可以看做是孔子所提倡的学习方法。

③ 启蒙时代或启蒙运动,又称理性时代,是指发生在17、18世纪欧洲的一场反封建、反教会的资产阶级思想文化解放运动,它为资产阶级革命做了思想准备和舆论宣传,是继文艺复兴运动之后欧洲近代第二次思想解放运动。其核心就是用理性之光驱散黑暗,把人们引向光明,积极地批判专制主义和宗教愚昧,宣传自由、平等和民主。

④ Voltaire:伏尔泰(1694—1778),法国启蒙思想家、文学家、哲学家。

Words and Expressions for Confucian Educational Theory
孔子教育理念相关英语词汇和表达式

learning at the government hall	学在官府
learning for all hierarchical levels and for all ages	有教无类
the "Six Arts" — ritual, music, archery, chariot-riding, calligraphy, and computation	六艺：礼乐射御书数
poetry and rites	诗礼
Revise the old in order to deduce new things.	温故知新
Learning and thinking are equally important.	学思并重
Learn in a systematic and progressive way, from a beginner's level to the advanced.	循序渐进
Inspiration and Guidance	启发诱导
Teach according to students' ability; use the appropriate material for teaching.	因材施教

Difficult Sentences

① Confucius broke the rule of "Xue Zai Guan Fu" (learning at the government hall). He encouraged "learning for all hierarchical levels and for all ages", and opened the door of education to the commoners.
孔子打破"学在官府"的陈规。他鼓励"有教无类"，向普通人打开了教育的大门。

② He said, "If one does not learn poetry, one will not be able to talk properly", "If one does not learn rites, one will never be well footed in the society."
子曰："不学诗，无以言"；"不学礼，无以立"。

③ Confucius's goal is to create gentlemen who carry themselves with grace, speak correctly, and demonstrate integrity in all things.
孔子的目的是培养举止优雅、言谈得体、遇事周全的谦谦君子。

④ His pedagogical methods are striking. He posed questions, cited passages from the classics, or used apt analogies, and waited for his students to arrive at the right answers. He said, "I only instruct the eager and enlighten the fervent. If I hold up one corner and a student cannot come back to me with the other three, I do not go on with the lesson."
孔子很讲究教育方法。他提出问题，或引经据典，或巧妙使用类比，启发学生自己得出结论。他认为，"不愤不启，不悱不发。举一隅不以三隅反，则不复也。"

Exercises

Task 1 Thinking and Judging

Directions: *Read Text 1 & 2 and judge whether the following statements are true (T) or false (F).*

True *if the statement agrees with the information mentioned in the passage.*

False *if the statement contradicts the information mentioned in the passage.*

(   ) (1) Chinese education has a long history dating from the Xia, Shang and Zhou dynasties 3,000/4,000 years ago.

(   ) (2) Education became more popular by the Spring and Autumn/Warring States period.

(   ) (3) Mencius became the earliest founder for "Private Education" for the sake of his mother.

(   ) (4) The curriculum at private schools was based on the Confucian Five Classics.

(   ) (5) Translations of Confucian texts influenced European thinkers of the 17th century Europe.

Task 2 Reading Comprehension

Directions: *Read Text 2 and answer the following questions by selecting one correct answer from A, B, C, or D for each question.*

(1) The connection between Confucius and _____ became permanently linked right into the present time.
   A. Academy education
   B. the official Chinese educational system
   C. public education
   D. private school

(2) Who had been regarded as the pioneer founder of family education?
   A. Laozi   B. Confucius   C. Mencius   D. Zhuangzi

(3) Before private education began, only _____ could be taught in government schools.
   A. government officials   B. noblemen's children
   C. Confucian scholars   D. children of the rich

(4) Which is the correct translation of the sentence: Learning without thought is labor lost; thought without learning is perilous(危险的)?
   A. 有教无类。   B. 学而时习之，不亦说乎？
   C. 温故知新。   D. 学而不思则罔，思而不学则殆。

(5) Which French philosopher was influenced by Confucius, who portrayed China as a model for Europe?
   A. Montesquieu   B. Hugo   C. Voltaire   D. Balzac

Task 3　Translating

Directions: *Translate the following expressions into English.*

(1) 温故知新

(2) 学思并重

(3) 循序渐进

(4) 启发诱导

(5) 因材施教

Task 4　Discussing and Writing

Nowadays more and more people tend to send their children to a private academy（书院）for a traditional education. What are the advantages and disadvantages of a private academy in your opinion? Discuss with your classmates about this issue and write a composition of more than 150 words to state your point of view.

Section B　Listening and Speaking

Text 3　Situational Dialogue: On Chinese Imperial Examination

(*Michael, an American student learning Chinese in China; Zhang, a Chinese teacher*)

Z: How are you doing recently?

M: I'm reading a book on ancient Chinese education, and the Imperial Education（科举）is mentioned here, something I'm not very clear about. Would you tell me more about it?

Z: My pleasure. The Chinese Imperial Examination was an examination system in Imperial China designed to select talented people for future positions in civil service. This system had a huge influence on both society and culture in Imperial China.

M: So it must have a long history and great impact?

Z: Yes. It was established in 605 during the Sui Dynasty and lasted more than 1300 years until the last examination in 1904 when the last Chinese feudal kingdom—the Qing Dynasty—was coming to an end. Somehow the modern examination system for selecting civil service staff also indirectly evolved from the imperial one.

M: Could you explain it in detail?

Z: ①It was part of the process by which candidates who passed the exams could receive a title called jinshi（进士）, or some other degree, which in turn would generally be followed by appointments to government offices. The first three of Jinshi were ranked Zhuangyuan（状元）, Bangyan（榜眼）and Tanhua（探花）respectively.

M: What are the forms of the examinations?

Z: The examinations consisted of a battery of tests(一系列的测试) administered at the district, provincial, and imperial levels. Only three hundred candidates could pass the imperial examinations, which would be supervised by the emperor himself. Candidate scholars often took the examinations several times before earning a degree.

M: How long did the exam last?

Z: Each exam taker spent three days and two nights writing "eight-legged essays" — literary compositions with eight distinct sections — in a tiny room with a makeshift(简易的) bed, a desk, and a bench. There were no interruptions in those three days, nor were candidates allowed any communication.

M: How did examiners evaluate the examinations?

Z: Since the pressure to succeed was intense, cheating and corruption were rampant(猖獗). In order to obtain objectivity in evaluation, candidates were identified by number rather than name, and examination answers were recopied by a third person before being evaluated to prevent the candidates' handwriting from being recognized.

M: Then who could take part in the exams?

Z: In the ancient society, class consciousness was strong and many people from lower classes would have had little chance to reach high office, not to mention having any position in the official court. However, once the imperial examination system was introduced, any male adult in China, regardless of his wealth or social status, could become a high-ranking government official by passing the imperial examination and thus realize his self-development. In this sense, passing the imperial examination was also called "carps jumping across the dragon's gate"（鲤鱼跳龙门）. ②The dragon had always been regarded as the symbol of mighty power and especially that of the rights exercised by the emperor; consequently the success of examination candidates was proudly called "jumping across the dragon's gate."

M: So what were the functions of the exam?

Z: In imperial China, the examination system and associated methods of recruitment to the central bureaucracy were major mechanisms(机制) by which the central government captured and held the loyalty of local-level elites(精英). ③The examination system also served to maintain cultural unity and consensus on basic values. The uniformity(一致) of the content of the examinations meant that the local elites and ambitious would-be members of those elites across China were taught with the same values.

M: It must have far-reaching influence?

Z: Yes. Despite the significant effect of promoting Confucian culture and education, it also influenced education systems in many other countries like Korea, Japan, and Vietnam, and similarities can be found in the personnel selection methods employed in France, America and Britain. Today's education system is surely its successor.

M: So this imperial examination system actually survives and even thrives in modern times!
Z: You bet! (671 words)
(Based on http://en.wikipedia.org/wiki/Imperial_examination)

The imperial examination cubicles, Koong Yuin, Canton, c. 1875

Words and Expressions for Chinese Imperial Examination
中国古代科举制度相关英语词汇和表达方式

Chinese Imperial Examination	中国古代科举制度
a battery of tests	一系列的测试
eight-legged essay	八股文
district examination	乡试
provincial examination	会试
Palace Examination/the final imperial examination	殿试

Difficult Sentences

① It was part of the process by which candidates who passed the exams could receive a title called jinshi（进士）, or some other degree, which in turn would generally be followed by appointments to government offices.
通过科举考试的举子可以得到"进士"头衔，或者别的衔号，下一步通常就可能就任官职。

② The dragon had always been regarded as the symbol of mighty power and especially that of the rights exercised by the emperor, consequently the success of examination candidates was proudly called "jumping across the dragon's gate."
"龙"是强权尤其是王权的象征，因此，考取功名被誉为"跳龙门"。

③ The examination system also served to maintain cultural unity and consensus on basic value.
科举制度同时也维持了文化的统一和基本价值观的一致。

Text 4 An Introduction to China Ancient Academies（书院）

China Ancient Academy, also called Shu Yuan, is a unique education institution in ancient China. It was born roughly in the Tang Dynasty and thrived in the Song Dynasty and popularized in the Ming and Qing Dynasties. Since the late Qing Dynasty, some of these ancient academies had been reconstructed into modernized colleges or universities.

China Ancient Academy exists in China for more than 1,000 years. ①It makes great contributions to the succession and popularity of Chinese culture as well as diversities of theories and heritages. A lot of ancient thinkers were educated in such a form of educational sectors.

②The Academy used to be founded by individuals, and in some dynasties it was owned by states by virtue of purchasing, donation and exchange.

Today many people say Europe is the origin land of modern university; it is right, but not absolutely. Ancient Chinese academy could be regarded as the earliest to carry out higher education as far as university education and mechanism are concerned.

The most famous four ancient Chinese academies include: Yuelu Academy, White-Deer Grotto Academy, Yingtian Academy and Songyang Academy.

◆ **Yuelu Academy（岳麓书院）**

Yuelu Academy

The Yuelu Academy is located on the east side of Yuelu Mountain in Changsha, the capital of Hunan Province, on the west bank of the Xiang River. It was established in 976 A.D at the time of the Northern Song Dynasty. The academy accepted disciples（门徒）throughout the Song, Yuan, Ming and Qing Dynasties. It was only in 1903 that the academy was transformed from a school of traditional Confucian learning to an institute of higher learning, and in 1926 it was officially named Hunan University.

Early in 1015, Emperor Zhen Zong of the Song Dynasty（宋真宗）awarded the academy his Majesty's own handwriting "Yuelu Academy" on a tablet（牌匾）. From then on many famous scholars and great thinkers gave lectures there; among them were Zhang Shi①, Zhu Xi② and WangYangming③.

Most of the existing Yuelu Academy buildings were constructions of the Ming and

---

① 张栻(1133—1180), 南宋著名理学家和教育家, 湖湘学派集大成者。与朱熹、吕祖谦齐名, 时称"东南三贤"。官至右文殿修撰。著有《南轩集》。

② 朱熹(1130—1200), 南宋著名的理学家、思想家、哲学家、教育家、诗人、闽学派的代表人物。

③ 王阳明(1472—1529), 明代著名思想家、教育家、文学家、书法家、哲学家和军事家。他是陆王心学之集大成者, 非但精通儒、释、道三教, 而且能够统军征战, 是中国历史上罕见的全能大儒。

Qing Dynasties. In 1956 the academy was listed as a historical site at the provincial level and later, in 1988 it became a historical site at the state level.

The academy has witnessed more than a thousand years of history and is the only one of the ancient Chinese academies of Classical Learning to have evolved into a modern institution of higher education.

◆ **White Deer Grotto Academy(白鹿洞书院)**

The White Deer Grotto Academy was located at the foot of Wulou Peak in Lushan, Jiangxi Province. Having fallen into ruin, it was rebuilt by the prominent neo-Confucianist Zhu Xi during the Southern Song Dynasty and reopened in 1180. It became an important center of Confucian thought during the following eight centuries. Zhu Xi himself taught there during the Southern Song as did Wang Yangming during the Ming Dynasty.

The White Deer Grotto Academy

The rules of the academy as set down by Zhu Xi had a profound and lasting influence on the subsequent development of Confucianism.

◆ **Yingtian Academy(应天书院)**

The beginnings of Yingtian Academy reached back to the times of the Later Jin(后晋 936—946). It was also called Suiyang Academy(睢阳书院). The first designation(名称) was derived from the Tang Dynasty (618—907) for the sake of the name of the city of Suiyang(今天的河南商丘), where the academy was located. ③ In 1006 the city was elevated to the status of prefecture(府) with the name of Yingtian(应天), and in 1014 it was given the designation of Southern Capital (Nanjing); that's the reason why the Academy was also called Academy of the Southern Capital(南京书院). In 1035 the Academy was transformed into a prefectural school(府学) and in 1043 it was made the Directorate of Education(国子监) of the Southern Capital. It occupied an important role in the educational system of the Northern Song period (960—1126).

In 1126 the buildings were destroyed by Jurchen(女真) troops during their invasion of northern China, and the school fell into decay. Only during the Ming Dynasty (1368—1644) in 1531, a censor(御使) named Cai Ai(蔡瑷) reorganized the school and gave it the name Yingtian Academy(应天书院). It ceased to function as a school after 1579.

The curriculum of the Academy included the Confucian Classics, historiography(历史编纂学), Yin-Yang teaching(阴阳学), astronomy(天象学), and philology(文献学).

◆ **Songyang Academy(嵩阳书院)**

At the foot of Mt. Songshan where Shaolin Temple, the cradle-land of Chinese Kungfu, is located, the Songyang Academy was first built in the 8th year (484) of

Emperor Wei Xiao's reign(北魏孝文帝) of the Northern Wei Dynasty (386—534).

The building of the academy is old and elegant. There are over 100 rooms covering more than 10,000 square meters.

Songyang Academy

Many emperors came here in a tour of inspection. In the Song Dynasty, it came to fame when Cheng Hao and Cheng Yi ①, the representatives of Neo-Confucianism (新儒学;道学) and the creators of Theory of Luo (it is said to be one of the origins of Taiji Kungfu) made speeches there. The Academy also attracted many famous scholars or masters to come and make lectures such as Sima Guang②, Fan Zhongyan③, and Zhu Xi. Hundreds of scholars came here as students and followers of these great Confucian thinkers. (886 words)

[Based on http://www.newworldencyclopedia.org/entry/Academies_(Shuyuan)
http://history.cultural-china.com/en/168 History9,365.html
http://www.chinaknowledge.de/History/history.htm
http://www1.chinaculture.org/library/2008-01/16/content_38,994.htm]

Words and Expressions for the Academies
中国古代书院相关英语词汇和表达方式

the Academy (of Classical Learning)	中国古代书院
private research and educational institutions	私立教学研究机构
the compilation and study of classical literature	编辑研究古籍
Confucianism and Neo-Confucianism	儒学和新儒学
the Songyang Academy	嵩阳书院
The Yingtian Academy	应天书院
The Yuelu Academy	岳麓书院
The White Deer Grotto Academy	白鹿洞书院

---

① 程颢(1032—1085),北宋哲学家、教育家。人称明道先生,与其弟程颐(1033—1107)同为宋代理学的主要奠基者,世称"二程"。因二程兄弟长期讲学于洛阳,故世称其学为"洛学"。二程在哲学上建立了以"天理"为核心的唯心主义理学体系。他和程颐的学说后来为朱熹所继承和发挥,世称程朱学派。著作收入《二程全书》。

② 司马光(1019—1086),北宋政治家、文学家、史学家,著有史学巨著《资治通鉴》。

③ 范仲淹(989—1052),北宋著名的政治家、思想家、军事家和文学家,世称"范文正公"。

Unit 4

Education in Ancient China

The Donglin Academy	东林书院
Directorate of Education	国子监
Luoyang school	洛学

Difficult Sentences

① It makes great contributions to the succession and popularity of Chinese culture as well as diversities of theories and heritages.

(书院)对中国文化的传承和传播做出了巨大贡献,同时也推动了文化理论和文化遗产的多样化。

② The Academy used to be founded by individuals, and in some dynasties it was owned by states by virtue of purchasing, donation and exchange.

书院曾经属于个人私有,在有些朝代通过购买、捐赠和交换的方式成为国有书院。

③ In 1006 the city was elevated to the status of prefecture with the name of Yingtian, and in 1014 it was given the designation of Southern Capital (Nanjing); that's the reason why the Academy was also called Academy of the Southern Capital.

1066年,这个城市升级为"府",改名"应天";1044年又成为南都建制,这就是为什么该书院被称为"南京书院"的原因。

Exercises

Task 1 Thinking and Judging.

Directions: *Read Text 3 and judge whether the following statements are true (T) or false (F).*

(　　) (1) The Imperial Examination (科举) was an examination system in Imperial China designed to select talented people for future positions in civil service.

(　　) (2) The Imperial Examination lasted more than 1300 years from the Tang Dynasty to the late Qing Dynasty.

(　　) (3) The Imperial Examination evaluation system enabled any adult in China, regardless of his wealth or social status, to become a high-ranking government official by passing the imperial examination.

(　　) (4) The uniformity of the content of the examinations meant that the local elites and ambitious would-be members of those elites across China could appreciate creativity and diversity.

(　　) (5) The modern examination system for selecting civil service staff can find some hints in the imperial one.

Task 2 Reading Comprehension

Directions: *Read Text 4 and answer the following questions by selecting one correct answer from A, B, C, or D for each question.*

(1) China Ancient Academies existed in Chinese history _____.

  A. for about 2,000 years

  B. for more than 1,000 years

  C. ever since Confucius

  D. from the Tang Dynasty to the Ming Dynasty

(2) As far as university education and mechanism are concerned, _____ could be regarded as the earliest to carry out higher education.

  A. European Universities   B. ancient Chinese academies

  C. extended family schools   D. Confucius private schools

(3) Which is NOT one of the Four Great Academies?

  A. Songyang Academy   B. Yingtian Academy

  C. Yuelu Academy   D. Donglin Academy

(4) Which is the only one academy that evolved into a modern institution of higher learning?

  A. Donglin Academy   B. Yingtian Academy

  C. Yuelu Academy   D. White Deer Grotto Academy

(5) Which academy was rebuilt by Zhu Xi and became an important center of Confucian thought?

  A. Songyang Academy   B. Donglin Academy

  C. Yuelu Academy   D. White Deer Grotto Academy

Task 3 Vocabulary Building

Directions: *Complete the following sentences with the words listed below. Change the forms if necessary.*

set	institution	survived	evolved	reign
located	witnessed	founded	prestigious	lectured

  The Yuelu Academy is __(1)__ on the east side of Yuelu Mountain in Changsha, the capital of Hunan province, China, on the west bank of the Xiang River. It was __(2)__ in 976, the 9th year of the Song Dynasty under the __(3)__ of Emperor Kaibao. The Confucian scholars Zhu Xi and Zhang Shi both __(4)__ at the academy.

  As one of the four most __(5)__ academies over the last 1000 years in China, Yuelu Academy has been a famous __(6)__ of higher learning as well as a centre of academic activities and cultures since it was formally __(7)__ up in 976 (during the Northern Song

Unit 4

Education in Ancient China

Dynasty). The Academy, which has ___(8)___ the Song, Yuan, Ming and Qing Dynasties, was later renamed Hunan University in 1926.

The academy has ___(9)___ more than a thousand years of history and is the only one of the ancient Chinese academies of Classical Learning to have ___(10)___ into a modern institution of higher learning.

Task 4 Listening and Speaking

Directions: *Listen to the dialogue in Text 3 twice and summarize the main points about ancient Chinese Imperial Examination. Then introduce it to foreign friends in your own words.*

Translation Practice

Directions: *Translate the following passages into English.*

（1）中国古代教育在中国文化中起着举足轻重的作用。中国古代教育最早可以追溯到周朝中后期诸子百家的教育思想。古代中国的教育给人们提供了一个平等的发展机会，即使出身贫寒的人也有可能步入仕途。春秋时期，伟大的教育家孔子打破"学在官府"的陈规，私人学堂盛行。不同的学派通过学堂传播他们的思想主张，出现了百花齐放、百家争鸣的局面。

（2）孔子既是教育家又是哲学家。他的思想理论规范影响着人们的伦理、道德、生活等方方面面。孔子思想的特征之一是他十分强调教育与学习。在思与学的关系上，他认为学思并重。他认为，"学而不思则罔，思而不学则殆。"对孔子来说，道德教育是最重要的。

Key to Unit 4 Exercises

Before You Start

1. What do you know about the ways ancient Chinese people received education?

In ancient China, people could go to a state-owned school for education, or to a private school（私塾）for studies. Some children would receive education at home by their parents or other relatives. Some families might invite a private teacher to teach their children alone.

2. What was the purpose of the Imperial Examination（科举考试）of ancient China?

The purpose of the Imperial Examination of ancient China was to select talented scholars as government officials. Culturally, the examination was intended to maintain Confucian teachings and manage intellectuals' thoughts and ideas.

3. How many famous ancient Chinese academies do you know? What are they?

岳麓（今湖南善化岳麓山）书院、白鹿洞（今江西庐山）书院、嵩阳（今河南登封）书院、应天(今河南商丘)书院合称中国古代四大书院。除此之外,还有江苏无锡的东林书院,湖南衡阳的石鼓书院,山东泰山的徂徕书院等。

Section A Reading and Writing

Task 1 Thinking and Judging

TTFFT

Task 2 Reading Comprehension

BBBDC

Task 3 Translating

温故知新(Revise the old in order to deduce new things.)

学思并重(Learning and thinking are equally important.)

循序渐进(Learn in a systematic and progressive way, from a beginner's level to the advanced)

启发诱导(Inspiration and Guidance)

因材施教(Teach according to students' ability; use appropriate materials for teaching.)

Task 4 Dicussing and Writing

Sample Writing

On Private Academy Education

People attach great importance to education all around the world. "Knowledge is power", as Sir Francis Bacon put it in a concisely accurate way. To receive a good education means to be powered by great knowledge. No wonder Chinese parents are willing to exert every effort to grant their children opportunities to enter an excellent high school and then a top university for schooling. However, there are parents who would rather send their children to a private academy to receive a traditional learning of Chinese classics. Why is it that they prefer traditional private teaching to modern public schooling?

In my point of view, a private academy enjoys many advantages compared to public schooling. In an academy, children are taught Chinese classics, such as works of Confucius, Mencius and Lao Tzu. There is no denying that such classical works embody the cream(精华) of traditional Chinese culture and convey great wisdom of Chinese philosophers. A serious learner may savor the thoughts inlaid in these enlightening books and obtain a tranquil perspective toward the world. Besides, the language of ancient Chinese classics is concise, elegant and profound. By reading philosophical works, novels and poetry, children will find their aesthetic senses highly refined. It is such works and learning that make us Chinese people what we are.

Of course, private academy education has its disadvantages, too. Above all, it cannot catch up with the times. In a globalized society, science and technology are valued as power of knowledge. Unfortunately, there is little advanced science or technology in ancient Chinese classics. If progress means keeping up with the developed countries, a private academy will never lead her students to a westernized way. This is why few people can stay in a private academy for a long education. It is really an old-fashioned way of education.

Out of fashion or not, private academies attract people for their classic taste and nostalgic curriculum. They may never replace public schools, but they will survive modernized civilization by adhering to the core values of Chinese thought, which, no matter how times change, will never vanish in Chinese culture. (354 words)

Section B Listening and Speaking

Task 1　Thinking and Judging
TFFFT

Task 2　Reading Comprehension
BBDCD

Task 3　Vocabulary Building
(1) located　　(2) founded　　(3) reign　　(4) lectured　　(5) prestigious
(6) institution　(7) set　　　(8) survived　(9) witnessed　(10) evolved

Task 4　Listening and Speaking
Omitted

参 考 译 文

(1) Education played a vital role in ancient Chinese culture. The origin of ancient Chinese education could date back to the educational ideas of the "Hundred Schools of Thought" in the middle and late Zhou Dynasty. It provided people with equal chance for development. Individuals from even the humblest backgrounds could rise to a higher level. In the Spring and Autumn Period, Confucius, the great educator, broke the rule of learning at the government hall. Private schools prevailed(流行,盛行)and many scholars of different schools of thought spread their teaching in this way and this led to the flourishing and contending of hundreds of schools.

(2) Confucius was an educator as well as a philosopher. His thoughts and theories had an impact on people in many aspects such as ethics, moral principles and rules of life. One of the features of Confucius's thoughts is his emphasis on education and learning. In the relationship between learning and thinking, he believed that learning and thinking were equally important. He believed that, "Learning without thought is labor lost; thought without learning is perilous(危险的)." He considered moral education the most important.

Unit 5

Science and Technology

导 读

本单元旨在通过对中国四大发明和古代科学家的简要介绍，使学生了解中国古代科学技术的杰出成就及其对世界文明发展的贡献；在此基础上学会相关的语言表达方式，从而在对外交流中能够熟练运用所学知识，宣传中华民族科学技术的发展进程及其对人类社会的贡献，让中国走向世界，让世界了解中国。

Before You Start

While you are preparing for this unit, think about the following questions:
1. Have you ever heard the Four Great Inventions before? What are they exactly?
2. Can you name any ancient Chinese scientists? What are their achievements respectively?

Section A Reading and Writing

Text 1 The Four Great Inventions

The Four Great Inventions refer to the inventions of paper, printing, compass and dynamite, which were among the most important Chinese technological advances, only known in Europe by the end of the Middle Ages. They are the major representatives among the numerous inventions by the ancient Chinese people.

Papermaking（造纸术）

Papermaking has traditionally been traced to China about 105 AD. ① According to historical records, Cai Lun in the Eastern Han Dynasty was the first person who, using such materials as bark, hards, rags and old fishnet, made what was to be termed as paper.

While paper is widely used worldwide today, the creator of this extremely important invention is little-known outside East Asia. After Cai invented paper in 105, it immediately

became widely used in China. In 751, some Chinese paper makers were captured by Arabs after Tang troops were defeated in the Battle of Talas River①. The techniques of papermaking then spread to the West.

Cai's contribution is considered one of the most important inventions in history, since it enabled China to develop its civilization much faster than with earlier writing materials (primarily bamboo), and it did the same with Europe when it was introduced in the 12th century or the 13th century.

Printing(印刷术)

- Block Printing(木刻版印刷)

With the inventions of paper and ink, stamper gradually became popular during the Jin Dynasty (265—420), which was the early form of Carved Type Printing. Block Printing first appeared in the Tang Dynasty (618—907). The text was first written on a piece of thin paper, then glued face down onto a wooden plate. The characters were carved out to make a wood-block(木版的) printing plate, which was used to print the text.

- Movable Type Printing(活字版印刷)

Block Printing was a costly and time-consuming process, for each carved block(印版) could only be used for a specific page of a particular book; besides, a single mistake in carving could ruin the whole block. However, movable type changed all of that.

In the Song Dynasty (960—1279), a man named Bi Sheng② carved individual characters on identical pieces of fine clay. ② Each piece of movable type had on it one

---

① 塔拉斯河是位于中亚的一条河流。怛罗斯战役(Battle of Talas,怛,音 dá)即爆发于塔拉斯河附近。该战役发生于唐玄宗天宝十年(751年),是唐朝的势力与初现在阿拉伯新兴阿拔斯王朝的势力在中亚诸国相遇而导致的战役。以唐军的失败而告终。怛罗斯之战是八世纪时最强大的东西方帝国间的碰撞,具有十分重大的历史意义。怛罗斯战役的一直接后果是推动了唐代中国高度发达的文明在西方世界的传播。

② 毕昇(？—1051),北宋著名发明家。宋仁宗庆历年间(1041—1048)发明了活字排版印刷术,这是印刷史上的一次伟大革命,它为我国文化经济的发展开辟了广阔的道路,为推动世界文明的发展作出了重大贡献。

Chinese character which was carved in relief(凸版的) on a small block of moistened clay. After the block had been hardened by fire, the type became hard and durable. The pieces of movable type could be used wherever required, and they could be glued to an iron plate and easily detached from the plate. Each piece of character could be assembled to print a page and then broken up and redistributed as needed. When the printing was finished, the pieces were put away for future use.

This technology then spread to Korea, Japan, Vietnam and Europe. Based on clay type, types made of wood, lead, tin and copper gradually appeared centuries later.

Dynamite(火药)

③Dynamite refers to a kind of mixture which has saltpeter(硝石), charcoal(木炭) and sulfur(硫黄) as its main components and can burn quickly or explode when lighted. Both saltpeter and sulfur are combustible(可燃的) and had served as medicine in ancient China, so they are called dynamite, which means "flaming medicine" in Chinese. In *Shen Nong Ben Cao Jing* (《神农本草经》), written in the Qin and Han Dynasties, the authors illustrated the medical characteristics of saltpeter and sulfur, and recorded the experimental results of smelting saltpeter. ④Qing Xuzi(清虚子) of the Tang Dynasty recorded the method dealing with dynamite powder in the course of alchemy(炼金术), which marked the real birth of the primitive dynamite powder. The alchemy and saltpeter of ancient China began to spread into the area of Arabia from the 8th or 9th century, while the production skills of dynamite powder weapons spread gradually first into Arabia and then into Europe from the 13th century on.

However, it was not until the 10th century or so that dynamite powder began to be used as a weapon.

The Compass(指南针)

⑤The compass is an instrument used to indicate directions with the help of magnetism. It can be any magnetic device using a needle to indicate the direction of the magnetic north of a planet's magnetosphere. Compasses were initially used in Fengshui(风水) in ancient China. The earliest record of use of magnetic lodestone(天然磁石) as a direction point was in a 4th century BC Chinese book: *Book of the Devil Valley Master* (《鬼谷子》).

⑥*Dream Pool Essays* (《梦溪笔谈》) written by the Song Dynasty scholar Shen Kuo (沈括) in 1086 AD contained a detailed description of how geomancer(风水先生;堪舆师) magnetized a needle by rubbing its tip with lodestone, and hanged the magnetic needle with one single strain of silk with a bit of wax attached to the center of the needle.

Knowledge of the compass moved overland through the Arab countries and then to Europe sometime later in the 12th century. ⑦According to the historical records, the compass began to serve as an instrument for navigation in as early as the late 11th century and the early 12th century. In about 1180 the compass was brought into Europe via Arab. (833 words)

(Based on:《用英语说中国》,浩瀚、李生禄主编. 科学技术文献出版社,2007-12-1
http://en.wikipedia.org/wiki/Four_Great_Inventions)

Difficult Sentences

① According to historical records, Cai Lun in the Eastern Han Dynasty was the first person who, using such materials as bark, hards, rags and old fishnet, made what was to be termed as paper.
据史书记载,东汉人蔡伦最早发明以树皮、麻头、破布、旧渔网等为原料制作的纸。

② Each piece of movable type had on it one Chinese character which was carved in relief (凸版的) on a small block of moistened clay. After the block had been hardened by fire, the type became hard and durable and could be used wherever required
每块活体字模都是一个汉字,用凸版样式刻在一小块胶泥片上,一字一印,用火烧硬后,便成活字,坚固耐用,随用随取。

③ Dynamite refers to a kind of mixture which has saltpeter, charcoal and sulfur as its main components and can burn quickly or explode when lighted.
火药本指以硝石、硫黄、木炭等为主要成分、点火后能迅速燃烧或爆炸的一种混合剂。

④ Qing Xuzi of the Tang Dynasty recorded the method dealing with dynamite powder in the course of alchemy, which marked the real birth of the primitive dynamite powder.
唐朝清虚子关于在炼丹术中使用火药的文字记载,被认为是早期火药真正诞生的标志。

⑤ The compass is an instrument used to indicate directions with the help of magnetism. It can be any magnetic device using a needle to indicate the direction of the magnetic north of a planet's magnetosphere.
指南针是一种利用磁性指示方向的仪器,它可以指任何使用磁针指明行星磁层磁北方向的磁性装置。

⑥ *Dream Pool Essays* written by Song Dynasty scholar Shen Kuo in 1086 AD contained a detailed description of how geomancer magnetized a needle by rubbing its tip with lodestone, and hanged the magnetic needle with one single strain of silk with a bit of wax attached to the center of the needle.
宋代学者沈括在公元1086年所著的《梦溪笔谈》中详细描述了风水先生(地卜者)如何以磁石磨针锋使之磁化,在磁针中心粘些蜡,用丝线悬挂起来(制成指南针)。

⑦ According to the historical records, the compass began to serve as an instrument for navigation in as early as the late 11th century and the early 12th century. In about 1180 the compass was brought into Europe via Arabs.
现存史料记载,指南针早在11世纪末12世纪初就已用作海上导航设备了,1180年前后经阿拉伯传人欧洲。

Text 2　Shen Kuo and *Dream Pool Essays*

The *Dream Pool Essays* was an extensive book written by the Chinese polymath（博学者）, scientist and statesman Shen Kuo (1031—1095) by 1088 AD, during the Song Dynasty (960—1279) of China. Although Shen was previously a highly renowned government official and military general, he compiled this enormous written work while virtually isolated on his lavish（奢侈的）garden estate near modern-day Zhenjiang, Jiangsu Province. He named the book after the name he gave to his estate, the "Dream Pool".

沈　括

Shen Kuo's written work of *Dream Pool Essays* records various fields of study including geology, astronomy, movable type printing, botany and zoology, etc. He wrote about mineralogy（矿物学）, erosion, sedimentation（沉积学）and uplift, mathematics and meteorology（气象学）. ①Shen Kuo's immortal masterpiece *Dream Pool Essays*, in which the word "shiyou" (petroleum) was used for the first time in the literature of Chinese history, was his remarkable contribution to science. The book contains the first written description of the magnetic needle compass, the first description in China of experiments with camera obscura（暗箱）, the invention of movable type printing by the artisan Bi Sheng (990—1051), and the mathematical basis for spherical trigonometry（三角学）that would later be mastered by the astronomer and engineer Guo Shoujing①(1231—1316).

Shen Kuo discovered that compasses do not point true north but to the magnetic north pole. This was a decisive step to make them useful for navigation. ② While using a sighting tube of improved width to correct the position of the polestar（北极星）, which had shifted over centuries, Shen discovered the concept of true north and magnetic declination towards the North Magnetic Pole, a concept which would aid navigators in the years to come. ③He advocated that the solar calendar with thirty one or thirty days a month and "lichun" as beginning of the year be used to replace the lunar calendar.

④And in geography and geology, he built up the cubic model of the topography of the North Liao state and compiled the atlas of the North Song Dynasty. He formulated a

---

① 郭守敬(1231—1316)，中国元朝的天文学家、数学家、水利专家和仪器制造专家。1276年修订新历法，经4年时间制订出《授时历》，通行360多年。是当时世界上最先进的一种历法。1981年，为纪念郭守敬诞辰750周年，国际天文学会以他的名字为月球上的一座环形山命名。

hypothesis for the process of land formation; based on his observation of fossil shells in a geological stratum in a mountain hundreds of miles from the ocean, he inferred that the land was formed by erosion of the mountains and by deposition of silt.

Unlike most people in his time, Shen Kuo took an objective and speculative viewpoint on natural phenomena. He wrote an accurate description of the damaging effects of lightning to buildings and to the specific materials of objects within. One passage in *Dream Pool Essays* called "Strange Happenings" contains a peculiar account of an unidentified flying object (UFO). Shen wrote that, during the reign of Emperor Renzong (1022—1063), an object as bright as a pearl occasionally hovered over the city of Yangzhou at night, but it was described first by local inhabitants of eastern Anhui and then in Jiangsu. (496 words)

(Based on:《用英语说中国》,浩瀚、李生禄主编. 科学技术文献出版社,2007-12-1

http://en.wikipedia.org/wiki/Four_Great_Inventions

http://en.wikipedia.org/wiki/Dream_Pool_Essays)

Difficult Sentences

① Shen Kuo's immortal masterpiece *Dream Pool Essays*, in which the word "shiyou" (petroleum) was used for the first time in the literature of Chinese history, was his remarkable contribution to science.

他的不朽名著《梦溪笔谈》,为科学做出了卓越贡献。该书是中国历史上最早使用"石油"这一名称的著作。

② While using a sighting tube of improved width to correct the position of the polestar, which had shifted over centuries, Shen discovered the concept of true north and magnetic declination towards the North Magnetic Pole, a concept which would aid navigators in the years to come.

沈括使用扩展窥管来校正北极星的位置——其位置历经数百年已发生了变化——他提出了真北和磁偏角的概念,这对后来的航海家航海帮助很大。

③ He advocated that the solar calendar with thirty one or thirty days a month and "lichun" as beginning of the year be used to replace the lunar calendar.

他提出用阳历代替阴历的主张,立春为岁首,大月31天,小月30天。

④ And in geography and geology, he builds up the cubic model of the topography of the North Liao state and compiles the atlas of the North Song Dynasty.

在地理地质学方面,他制作了辽北立体地形模型,编制了北宋疆域地形图。

Exercises

Task 1 Reading Comprehension

Directions: *Decide whether the following statements are TRUE or FALSE according to Text 1.*

(   ) (1) Cai Lun was credited as the first person who, using such materials as bark, hards, rags and old fishnet, made what was to be termed as paper.

(   ) (2) Before the invention of paper, earlier writing materials were quite heavy and inconvenient.

(   ) (3) Block Printing was a costly and time-consuming process, for each carved block could only be used for a specific page of a particular book.

(   ) (4) Dynamite originally had served as medicine in ancient China, by Chinese alchemists searching for immortality, but it was not until the 10th century or so that dynamite powder began to be used as a weapon.

(   ) (5) Compasses were initially used in Fengshui in ancient China, which was recorded in *Dream Pool Essays*.

Task 2 Vocabulary Building

Directions: *Complete the following sentences with the words listed below. Change the forms if necessary.*

| initial | formulate | represent | advocate | reign |
| hover | masterpiece | redistribute | decide | introduce |

(1) The _____ of Zhu Yuanzhang lasted about 31 years.

(2) A hawk _____ in the sky.

(3) We should _____ a long-term program for scientific and technological development.

(4) Shen Kuo's discovery of magnetic north pole was a _____ step to make it useful for navigation.

(5) He is a(n) _____ of more airplanes and fewer warships.

(6) Jiuzhaigou is the _____ of nature.

(7) Compasses were _____ used in feng shui in ancient China.

(8) Each piece of movable character could be assembled to print a page and then broken up and _____ as needed.

(9) It was not until the 12th century or the 13th century that paper-making was _____ to Europe.

(10) The Four Great Inventions are the major _____ among the numerous inventions by the ancient Chinese people.

Unit 5 Science and Technology

Task 3 Translating

Directions: *Translate the following part of* Dream Pool Essays *into Chinese.*

The clothing of China since the Northern Qi (550—557) onward has been entirely made barbarian. Narrow sleeves, short dark red or green robes, tall boots and metal girdle ornaments are all barbarian garb. The narrow sleeves are useful when shooting while galloping. The short robes and tall boots are convenient when passing through tall grass. The barbarians all enjoy thick grass as they always sleep in it. I saw them all do it when I was sent north. Even the king's court is in the deep grasses. On the day I had arrived at the barbarian court the new rains had passed and I waded through the grass. My robes and trousers were all soaked, but the barbarians were not at all wet.

Section B Listening and Speaking

Text 3 Situational Dialogue: Xu Guangqi

(H: *Howard, an American student learning Chinese in China*; L: *Li Ping, a Chinese student*)

H: I was told that Xu Guangqi was a pioneer of introducing Western scientific achievements in China. Thus I am quite interested in this figure.

L: That's right. Xu Guangqi (1562—1633) was a Chinese agricultural scientist and mathematician born in Shanghai. ①He was also the first intellectual believer in Catholicism in the late Ming Dynasty (1368—1644) as well as a top official.

Xu Guangqi (right) & Matteo Ricci (left)

H: Amazing! How did Xu get in contact with the Catholicism, which was originally a western religion?

L: Well, in 1595, he got to know several foreign missionaries in Guangzhou. ②In 1600, when he was on his way to Beijing for the Imperial Examination(科举考试), he met Matteo Ricci①(利玛窦) for the first time in Nanjing, and admired the latter's knowledge.

H: I've read about Matteo Ricci, who was called Li Madou in Chinese history books. Matteo Ricci was born in 1552 in Italy. Ricci started learning theology and law in a Roman Jesuit school, and in 1577 he applied for a missionary expedition to India. In August 1582, Ricci arrived at Macau, a Portuguese trading post on the South China Sea.

---

① 利玛窦(1552—1610),天主教耶稣会意大利籍神父、传教士、学者。1583年来到中国居住,是天主教在中国传教的开拓者之一,也是第一位阅读中国文学并对中国典籍进行钻研的西方学者。他除传播天主教教义外,还广交中国官员和社会名流,传播西方天文、数学、地理等科学技术知识。他的著述对中西交流做出了重要贡献。

L: Indeed! Once in Macau, Ricci started learning Chinese language and customs. This was the beginning of a long project that made him one of the first Western scholars to master Chinese script and Classical Chinese.

H: That's true. With another missionary, he traveled to some major cities of mainland China, seeking to establish a permanent Jesuit mission outside Macau.

L: ③Then in 1603, Xu Guangqi acquainted another foreign missionary and got a brief idea of the Catholicism. Soon, he received baptism(洗礼) and converted to the Catholicism, getting the name of Paul.

H: That explains how Xu became a Catholic.

L: Right! ④The spread of Catholicism in China in the early ages owed much to some officials and intellectuals, especially Xu Guangqi.

H: But why was Xu perceived as a pioneer of introducing Western scientific achievements in China?

L: He liked the western science and technology and finished several translation works. Xu Guangqi was the first one who introduced European natural science to China and translated geometry into Chinese (six volumes of *Geometry Original*,《几何原本》). He was also the writer of *Nongzheng Quanshu* (*Complete Treatise on Agriculture*), one of the greatest agricultural books in China.

H: Tell me more about the masterpiece, please!

L: Sure! ⑤*Complete Treatise on Agriculture* consists of 12 phyla, 60 volumes, and altogether over 700 000 characters. As an agricultural encyclopedia, the book basically includes all the subjects concerned about almost all the domains in the life and production of ancient Chinese people, such as irrigation, farm tools, planting trees, herding, manufacturing, and silkworm breeding.

H: Great! I'll learn Chinese even harder and one day I'll read the book myself.

L: I'm sure you will. (496 words)

(Based on: http://en.wikipedia.org/wiki/Xu_Guangqi

http://www.chinaculture.org/created/2007-11/26/content_68,352.htm Complete Treatise on Agriculture)

Unit 5
Science and Technology

Difficult Sentences

① He was also the first intellectual believer in Catholicism in the late Ming Dynasty (1368—1644) as well as a top official.

他是明朝末年中国最早信奉天主教的文人,也是地位最高的官员。

② In 1600, when he was on his way to Beijing for the imperial examination, he met Matteo Ricci for the first time in Nanjing, and admired the latter's knowledge.

1600年徐光启到北京去参加科举考试,在路过南京时第一次与利马窦见面,非常钦佩他的学识。

③ In 1603, he acquainted another foreign missionary and got a brief idea of the Catholicism. Soon, he received baptism and converted to the Catholicism, getting the name of Paul.

1603年,他又认识了另一位传教士,了解了一些天主教教义。不久他受洗入教,取教名保罗。

④ The spread of Catholicism in China in the early ages owed much to some officials and intellectuals, especially Xu Guangqi.

天主教早期之所以能在中国传播,得力于一些中国政府官员和文人的帮助,其中最主要的就是徐光启。

⑤ *Complete Treatise on Agriculture* consists of 12 phyla, 60 volumes, and altogether over 700 000 characters. As an agricultural encyclopedia, the book basically includes all the subjects concerned about almost all the domains in the life and production of ancient Chinese people, such as irrigation, farm tools, planting trees, herding, manufacturing, and silkworm breeding.

《农政全书》分为12门,60卷,总计70余万字。作为一部农业百科全书,该书基本上囊括了诸如农田灌溉、农具制作、植树放牧及生产养蚕等古代农业生产和人民生活的各个方面。

Text 4 An Introduction to Zhaozhou Bridge

Ancient Chinese literature refers to the Zhaozhou Bridge as a "crescent moon rising from the clouds" or a "rainbow in the sky". Throughout its history, it has been known as the Anji Bridge(安济桥, literally "safe crossing"), the Dashi Bridge ("big stone").

The Zhaozhou Bridge crosses the Xiaohe River(洨河) in Zhaoxian County, Hebei Province. It is the country's oldest standing bridge and also the world's oldest open-spandrel arch bridge. ① There are two smaller arches at each end of the bridge that

---

① 敞肩型石拱桥,因桥两端肩部各有两个小孔,不是实的,故称敞肩型,这是世界造桥史上的一个创造,没有小拱的称为满肩或实肩型。

transmit the load of the deck(桥面) down to the main arch, which curves to form a shallow arch rather than the half circle preferred by Roman engineers at the time. The open spandrels allow some water to flow over the main arch when the river floods. This technique is a great innovation in the world's history of bridge engineering. ②Western scholars admit that the open-spandrel architecture of Zhaozhou Bridge is the predecessor of many modern structures made of reinforced concrete, ushering(开创) in a new style in bridge design.

Zhaozhou Bridge
The world's oldest and best-preserved stone arch bridge

The Zhaozhou Bridge was designed and constructed during the Sui Dynasty (581—618) by the master architect and stonemason(石匠), Li Chun. It is 50.82 meters long and 9.6 meters wide; the span(跨径,结构支承间的水平距离) of its large stone arch in the middle measures 37.37 meters—the world's largest arch at the time. It is comprised of 28 thin, curved limestone slabs, joined with iron dovetails(楔形榫头) so the arch could gently yield and adjust to the rise and fall of the abutments(拱座:承担拱顶重量或压力的部分) as they responded to the weight of traffic.

The bridge floor is smooth and flat with passages for pedestrians(行人) on both sides, while carriages and carts can move through the middle. ③The bridge is ingeniously designed, with a well-proportioned layout, solid structure and a magnificent and attractive outward appearance. Willow branches sway gracefully at both ends of the bridge and, from afar, the inverted image of the arch in the water resembles a rainbow spanning over the Xiaohe River.

The Zhaozhou Bridge is a wonder of architectural design for its ingenious design and beautiful decorations. However, it is even more remarkable because it has survived for centuries. ④In the past 1400 years, the bridge survived at least eight wars, ten major floods and numerous earthquakes, the most recent being the 7.2-magnitude Xingtai

Earthquake in 1966. Yet, the support structure remains intact and the bridge is still in use, making it one of the bridges with the longest service life in the world.

The Zhaozhou Bridge is by far the earliest and best preserved stone arch bridge in the world. ⑤It was listed by the State Council (国务院) in 1961 as one of the key cultural sites under national protection, and was also designated by the American Society of Civil Engineers (ASCE, 美国土木工程师学会) in 1991 as an International Historic Civil Engineering Landmark. In 1996, the Chinese authorities nominated it for inclusion in the World Heritage List as having "a very important place in the world bridge building history". (503 words)

(Based on: ASCE-American Society of Civil Engineering
http://www.asce.org/People-and-Projects/Projects/Landmarks/Zhaozhou-(or-Anji)-Bridge/
http://www.chinaculture.org/gb/en_travel
http://www.chinaculture.org/)

Difficult Sentences

① There are two smaller arches at each end of the bridge that transmit the load of the deck down to the main arch, which curves to form a shallow arch rather than the half circle preferred by Roman engineers at the time.
桥的两端各设两个小拱，从而使桥面的承重下移到主拱；主拱弯曲建成了扁弧形，而非当时罗马工匠所推崇的半圆形。

② Western scholars admit that the open-spandrel architecture of Zhaozhou Bridge is the predecessor of many modern structures made of reinforced concrete, ushering in a new style in bridge design.
西方学者承认，赵州桥的"敞肩型"建筑风格是众多现代化钢筋混凝土建筑的先驱，它开创了桥梁设计的新风尚。

③ The bridge is ingeniously designed, with a well-proportioned layout, solid structure and a magnificent and attractive outward appearance.
赵州桥不仅设计精巧，而且建造均衡对称，结构紧凑，气势宏伟，外观上十分美丽壮观。

④ In the past 1400 years, the bridge survived at least eight wars, ten major floods and numerous earthquakes, the most recent being the 7.2-magnitude Xingtai Earthquake in 1966.
赵州桥距今已1400年，经历了8次战乱，10次水灾和多次地震，最近的一次是1966年发生在邢台的7.2级地震。

⑤ It was listed by the State Council of China in 1961 as one of the key cultural sites under national protection, and was also designated by the American Society of Civil Engineers in 1991 as an International Historic Civil Engineering Landmark.
1961年赵州桥被中国国务院列为全国第一批重点文物保护单位；1991年又被美国土木工程师学会选定为（世界第十二处）"国际土木工程历史古迹"。

Exercises

Task 1 Listening and Speaking

Directions: *Listen to the dialogue carefully. Discuss with your classmates and answer the following questions.*

(1) How did Xu Guangqi convert to Catholicism, which was originally a western religion?

(2) Who was Matteo Ricci? How did he get acquainted with Xu Guangqi?

(3) Who was responsible for the spread of Catholicism in China in the early ages?

(4) Why was Xu perceived as a pioneer of introducing Western scientific achievements in China?

(5) What kind of book is *Nongzheng Quanshu* (*Complete Treatise on Agriculture*)?

Task 2 Listening Comprehension

Directions: *Listen to the lecture on Zhaozhou Bridge twice and take some notes, then complete the following statements by choosing the proper answer from A, B, C and D.*

(1) Zhaozhou Bridge leads the world in bridge construction because of its being _____.

　　A. the longest symmetrical arch bridge

　　B. the oldest stone-arched bridge

　　C. the oldest open-spandrel bridge

　　D. the best-proportioned bridge

(2) The length of Zhaozhou Bridge is _____ meters long.
   A. 50.82   B. 158.2   C. 150.8   D. 58.2
(3) The bridge's symmetrical arch structure not only requires fewer building materials but also helps relieve the damage of _____.
   A. wind   B. flood   C. rain   D. snowstorm
(4) The bridge's opening is shaped like _____, paying attention to both land and water transportation.
   A. a semicircle   B. a semi dome
   C. a smooth mirror   D. a bow
(5) Zhaozhou Bridge is even more remarkable because _____.
   A) it has survived for centuries
   B) it has survived several wars
   C) it has survived major floods and numerous earthquakes
   D) All of the above

Task 3 Vocabulary Building

Directions: *Complete the following sentences with the words listed below. Change the forms if necessary.*

innovation	symmetrical	influence	owe much to	expedition
a wide range of	design	intellectual	acquaint	domain

(1) Xu Guangqi was the first _____ believer in Catholicism in the late Ming Dynasty as well as a top official.
(2) The scientists will go on a(n) _____ to the South Pole.
(3) In 1603, Xu Guangqi _____ another foreign missionary and got a brief idea of the Catholicism.
(4) The spread of Catholicism in China in the early ages _____ some officials and intellectuals, especially Xu Guangqi.
(5) Both China and Russia are _____ countries in the world.
(6) The book of *Complete Treatise on Agriculture* covers _____ subjects.
(7) This question comes into the _____ of philosophy.
(8) Zhaozhou Bridge has smaller _____ arches built at each end, which protects the bridge mightily.
(9) The "open-spandrel" technique is a great _____ in the world's history of bridge engineering.
(10) There are efforts under way to _____ the bridge as a historic landmark.

Translation Practice

Directions: *Translate the following passages into English.*

(1) 沈括是宋朝的著名官员、军事将领。他的不朽名著《梦溪笔谈》(*Dream Pool Essays*)记载了包括地质学、天文学、活字印刷(movable type printing)、植物学和动物学等各种学科。该书是中国历史上最早使用"石油"这一名称的著作,为自然科学做出了卓越贡献。沈括与当时的大多数人不同,他以一种客观而思辨的态度观察自然现象。他提出了用阳历代替阴历的主张,立春为岁首,大月31天,小月30天。

(2) 徐光启(1562年~1633年)是中国明朝的数学家和农业科学家。他身为政府高官,最早将西方科技成就引入中国,也是明朝末年最早信奉天主教的文人。天主教早期之所以在中国传播,得力于一些中国政府官员和文人的帮助,特别是徐光启。徐光启撰写了《农政全书》(*Complete Treatise on Agriculture*)这部农业百科全书。该书基本上囊括了诸如农田灌溉、农具制作、植树、放牧、生产和养蚕等古代农业生产和人民生活的各个方面。

Words and Phrases Related to Science and Technology in Ancient China
中国古代科技相关词汇与表达方式

paper-making	造纸	hypothesis	假设
printing	印刷术	combustible	易燃的
compass	指南针	lunation	阴历月
dynamite/gunpowder	火药	approximation	近似值
block printing	木刻版印刷	polestar	北极星
movable type printing	活字印刷	equinox	春分或秋分
polymath	博学者	Catholicism	天主教
mathematician	数学家	missionary	传教士
astronomer	天文学家	functionary	职员,官员
erosion	腐蚀,侵蚀	*Dream Pool Essays*	《梦溪笔谈》
mineralogy	矿物学	*Complete Treatise on Agriculture*	《农政全书》
sedimentation	沉淀,沉降	*Geometry Original*	《几何原本》

Key to Unit 5 Exercises

Before You Start

1. Have you heard the Four Great Inventions before? What are they exactly?

Unit 5

Science and Technology

The Four Great Inventions refer to the inventions of paper, printing, compass and dynamite, which were among the most important Chinese technological advances. Papermaking has been traced to China about 105 AD, when Cai Lun in the Eastern Han Dynasty was the first person who, using such materials as bark, hards, rags and old fishnet, made what was to be termed as paper; Movable Type Printing was invented by a man named Bi Sheng in the Song Dynasty (960—1279); Dynamite was discovered in the 9th century by Chinese alchemists(炼金术士) searching for immortality, but it was not until the 10th century or so that dynamite powder began to be used as a weapon; Compasses, as an instrument used to indicate directions with the help of magnetism, were initially used in feng shui in ancient China. On the whole, the Four Great Inventions are the major representatives among the numerous inventions by the ancient Chinese people.

2. **Can you name any ancient Chinese scientists? What are the leading achievements in their own field?**

(For reference only)

张衡/Zhang Heng (78—139), was an astronomy, mathematician, and literary scholar as well as an inventor and artist in the Eastern Han Dynasty in China. In 132, Zhang invented the first seismograph (地震仪) for measuring earthquakes.

祖冲之/Zu Chongzhi (429—500), Chinese astronomer, mathematician, and engineer who created the Daming calendar and found several close approximations(近似值). As a mathematician, Zu Chongzhi's most remarkable achievement was the calculation of pi(圆周率的推算).

沈括/Shen Kuo (1031—1091), was a Chinese scientist, polymath, general, diplomat, and financial officer who was the recorder of compasses for navigation. Shen Kuo's immortal masterpiece *Dream Pool Essays*, in which the word "shiyou" (petroleum) was used for the first time in the literature of Chinese history, was his remarkable contribution to science.

徐光启/Xu Guangqi (1562—1633), was a Chinese agricultural scientist and mathematician born in Shanghai. His most influential work on science and technology was the immense book entitled *Complete Treatise on Agriculture*, consisting of 12 phyla, 60 volumes, and altogether over 700 000 characters.

Section A Reading and Writing

Task 1 **Reading Comprehension**
(1) T   (2) T   (3) T   (4) T   (5) F

Task 2 **Vocabulary Building**

(1) reign   (2) hovers   (3) formulate   (4) decisive
(5) advocate   (6) masterpiece (7) initially   (8) redistributed

(9) introduced   (10) representatives

Task 3 Translating

中国衣冠,自北齐以来,乃全用胡服。窄袖、绯绿短衣、长靿靴、有蹀躞带,皆胡服也。窄袖利于驰射,短衣、长靿皆便于涉草。胡人乐茂草,常寝处其间,予使北时皆见之。虽王庭亦在深荟中。予至胡庭日,新雨过,涉草,衣裤皆濡,唯胡人都无所沾。

Section B Listening and Speaking

Task 1 Listening and Speaking

(1) How did Xu Guangqi convert to Catholicism, which was originally a western religion?

Xu Guangqi got to know several foreign missionaries since 1595. Then in 1600 he met Matteo Ricci and from whom and another missionary he got some idea of Catholicism. Soon, he received baptism and converted to Catholicism, getting the name of Paul.

(2) Who was Matteo Ricci? How did he get acquainted with Xu Guangqi?

Matteo Ricci was called Li Madou in Chinese history books. He was one of the first Western scholars to master Chinese script and Classical Chinese. Ricci was born in 1552 in Italy. As a missionary, Ricci arrived at Macau in August 1582 and started learning Chinese language and customs. In 1600, Matteo Ricci met Xu Guangqi in Nanjing when Xu was on his way to Beijing for the imperial examination.

(3) Who was responsible for the spread of Catholicism in China in the early ages?

The spread of Catholicism in China in the early ages owed much to some officials and intellectuals, especially Xu Guangqi.

(4) Why was Xu perceived as a pioneer of introducing Western scientific achievements in China?

He liked western science and technology and finished several translation works. Xu Guangqi was the first one who introduced European natural science to China and translated geometry into Chinese (six volumes of *Geometry Original*).

(5) What kind of book is Nongzheng Quanshu (*Complete Treatise on Agriculture*)?

Complete Treatise on Agriculture is an agricultural encyclopedia, consisting of 12 phyla, 60 volumes, and altogether over 700 000 words. It covers a wide range of subjects, such as irrigation, farm tools, planting trees, herding, manufacturing, etc. The book basically includes all the subjects concerned about almost all the domains in the life and production of ancient Chinese people.

Task 2 Listening Comprehension

(1) C (2) A (3) B (4) D (5) D

Unit 5 Science and Technology

Task 3 Vocabulary Building

(1) intellectual　　(2) expedition　　(3) acquainted　　(4) owed much to
(5) influential　　(6) a wide range of　　(7) domain　　(8) symmetrical
(9) innovation　　(10) designate

参考译文

(1) Shen Kuo was a highly renowned government official and military general of the Song Dynasty. Shen Kuo's immortal masterpiece *Dream Pool Essays*《梦溪笔谈》records various fields of study including geology, astronomy, movable type printing, botany(植物学) and zoology, etc. In the book, the word "shiyou" (petroleum) was used for the first time in the literature of Chinese history, which was his remarkable contribution to science. Unlike most people in his time, Shen Kuo took an objective and speculative(思索性的) viewpoint on natural phenomena. He advocated that the solar calendar be used to replace the lunar calendar, with thirty-one or thirty days a month and "lichun" ("Start of Spring" according to lunisolar calendar"阴阳历") as the beginning of a year.

(2) Xu Guangqi (1562—1633) was a Chinese mathematician and agricultural scientist in the Ming Dynasty. As a top official, Xu was perceived as a pioneer introducing Western scientific achievements in China and also the first intellectual believer in Catholicism(天主教)in the late Ming Dynasty. The spread of Catholicism in China in the early ages owed much to some officials and intellectuals, especially Xu Guangqi. Xu compiled *Complete Treatise on Agriculture*《农政全书》, an agricultural encyclopedia(百科全书). The book basically includes all the subjects concerned about various domains in the life and production of ancient Chinese people, such as irrigation(灌溉), farm tool making, tree planting, herding, manufacturing, and silkworm breeding(养蚕).

Unit 6

Traditional Customs

导读

本单元旨在通过对传统婚庆礼仪、十二生肖、吉祥物和风水等中国古代习俗的简要介绍,使学生学会相关的文化知识和语言表达,加深对中华传统风土人情的理解,在对外交往中能更好地宣扬中华民族传统文化。

Before You Start

While you are preparing for this unit, think about the following questions:
1. Chinese culture is rich in traditional customs, such as marriage custom. Could you list traditional customs as many as you know?
2. What's the difference between traditional customs and superstitions? Please give an example.

Section A Reading and Writing

Text 1 Traditional Marriage Rituals

Chinese marriage became a custom between 402 B.C. and 221 B.C.. Despite China's long history and many different geographical areas, it was very important to follow a basic principle of Three Letters and Six Etiquettes ① in ancient times.

Three Letters

Three Letters include Betrothal Letter, Gift Letter and Wedding Letter. Betrothal Letter is the formal document of the engagement, a must in a marriage. Then a Gift Letter

---

① 三书六礼是中国的传统婚姻习俗礼仪。"三书"指在"六礼"过程中所用的文书,包括聘书、礼书和迎书。中国古代把婚礼过程分为六个阶段,古称"六礼",即纳采、问名、纳吉、纳征、请期、亲迎。

is necessary, which will be enclosed to the identified bride's family, listing types and quantity of gifts for the wedding once both parties accept the marriage. ①The Wedding Letter refers to the document which will be prepared and presented to the bride's family on the day of the wedding to confirm and commemorate the formal acceptance of the bride into the bridegroom's family.

Six Etiquettes are as follows:

◆ *Proposal*: ②When an unmarried boy's parents found a potential daughter-in-law, they then located a matchmaker whose job was to assuage(缓和) the conflict of interests and general embarrassments when discussing the possibility of marriage on the part of two families largely unknown to each other.

◆ *Birthdates*: ③If the selected girl and her parents did not object to the proposal, the matchmaker would match the birthdates in which Suan Ming (Chinese fortune telling) is used to predict the future of that couple-to-be. If the result of Suan Ming was good, they then would go to the next step, submitting bride price.

◆ *Betrothal gifts*(聘礼): At this point the bridegroom's family arranged for the matchmaker to present betrothal gifts, including the betrothal letter, to the bride's family.

◆ *Wedding gifts*: The groom's family would then send an elaborate array of food, cakes, and religious items to the bride's family.

◆ *Arranging the wedding*: Before wedding ceremony, two families would arrange a wedding day according to Chinese Tung Shing①(通胜). Selecting an auspicious(吉利的) day to assure a good future for the couple is as important as avoiding what is believed to be an unlucky day. In some cases there may be no auspicious dates and the couple will have to review their potential date range.

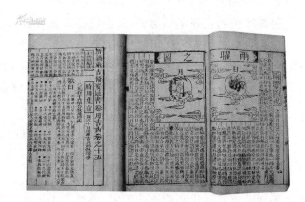

---

① 通胜即为旧时的黄历,主要内容为二十四节气的日期表,每天的吉凶宜忌、生肖运程等。本称"通书",但广东人认为"书"同"输"音,故取其反意,名之曰"通胜"。

◆ *Wedding ceremony*: On the selected day, the bridegroom departed with a troop of escorts(迎亲者) and musicians, who would play happy music all the way to the bride's home. After the bride was clustered to the bridegroom's home, the wedding ceremony began.

Unfortunately for some traditional families, the wife's mother could not go to her son-in-law's family until one year after the wedding had elapsed. However, during this year the daughter could go back at anytime.

Before modern times, women were not allowed to choose the person they married. Instead, the family of the bride picked the prospective husband. ④Marriages were chosen based upon the needs of reproduction and honor, as well as the need of the father and husband. (465 words)

(Based on: http://en.wikipedia.org/wiki/Chinese_marriage)

Difficult Sentences

① The Wedding Letter refers to the document which will be prepared and presented to the bride's family on the day of the wedding to confirm and commemorate the formal acceptance of the bride into the bridegroom's family.

迎书是指结婚当日呈献给新娘家的文书,以正式确认新娘过门到新郎家。

② When an unmarried boy's parents found a potential daughter-in-law, they then located a matchmaker whose job was to assuage(缓和) the conflict of interests and general embarrassments when discussing the possibility of marriage on the part of two families largely unknown to each other.

男方家长物色好了一女子,就会请媒人到女方家提亲。媒人会在不大相识的两家人联姻过程中起着中间人作用,以协调利益纷争,化解不便之处。

③ If the selected girl and her parents did not object to the proposal, the matchmaker would match the birthdates in which Suan Ming (Chinese fortune telling) is used to predict the future of that couple-to-be.

如女方家接纳男方家的提亲,媒人就会把双方的生辰八字交予算命先生以占卜凶吉。

④ Marriages were chosen based upon the needs of reproduction and honor, as well as the need of the father and husband.

婚姻是传宗接代和荣誉的需要,也是为了满足父亲和丈夫的需要。

Text 2   Traditional Chinese Mascots (吉祥物)

As an important part of Chinese traditional culture, Chinese traditional mascots represent human's aspiration to exorcise(驱赶) evil spirits and long for a happy life. The traditional representative mascots include the Chinese dragon and the Chinese phoenix.

Unit 6
Traditional Customs

The Chinese dragon is referred to as the divine creature that brings prosperity and good fortune. It is the ultimate representation of the forces of Mother Nature. Many legends drew connections between the dragon and the emperor, and some emperors claimed to have descended from dragon.

The Chinese dragon symbolizes power and excellence, valiancy(勇猛) and boldness, heroism and perseverance, nobility and divinity(神威). It is made up of nine entities, which include a head like a camel's, horns like a deer's, eyes like a hare's, ears like a bull's, a neck like a snake's, a belly like a frog's, scales(鳞) like a carp's(鲤鱼), paws like a tiger's, and claws like an eagle's.

The Chinese dragon has the ability to live in the seas, fly up the heavens and coil(盘绕) up in mountains. ①Being a divine animal, it can drive out wandering evil spirits, protect the innocent and bestow safety.

Because the Chinese dragon is looked upon as the symbol of good fortune, people have dragon dance to pray for good weather in order to achieve bumper harvest. ②Every 2nd of lunar February is the Dragon Raising Head Day in China. People would like to cut hair on that day for good luck. As a result, the Chinese dragon is an essential symbol of the spirit of Chinese nation and Chinese race itself. Dragon pattern is a traditional graphic for the Chinese people with rich cultural connotation and symbolic significance.

The Chinese phoenix, likewise, exists only in legends and fairy tales. Phoenix, also called firebird, is a Chinese mythical creature. In Chinese culture the phoenix is known as Fenghuang and is used to represent the empress. In Chinese folk custom, phoenix is regarded as the king of hundred birds, predicting luck, expressing love, driving evil, etc. It is the symbol of auspicious sign, imperial power and national culture. It is thought to be a gentle creature, which eats nothing but dewdrops.

Fenghuang is said to be made up of a beak(嘴,喙) of a rooster, a face of a swallow, a forehead of a fowl, a neck of a snake, a breast of a goose, a back of a tortoise, hindquarters of a stag(牡鹿) and a tail of a fish. ③The phoenix is often depicted in a pair with a male and a female facing each other, symbolizing a duality, the yin-yang, mutual interdependence in the universe. The male phoenix named "Feng" is the yang and solar, while the female one "Huang" is the yin and lunar. The Feng and the Huang together symbolize everlasting love, and as a bridal symbol signifying "inseparable fellowship".

④Down the ages, the Chinese dragon and the Chinese phoenix embedded with people's blessing and hope are the symbols of blissful relations between husband and wife, and common metaphors of yin and yang. (500 words)

Difficult Sentences

① Being a divine animal, it can drive out wandering evil spirits, protect the innocent and bestow safety.
作为神圣的动物,龙可以驱除邪灵鬼怪,保护无辜并护佑平安。

② Every 2nd of lunar February is the Dragon Raising Head Day in China.
在中国,农历的二月初二是龙抬头的日子。

③ The phoenix is often depicted in a pair with a male and a female facing each other, symbolizing a duality, the yin-yang, mutual interdependence in the universe.
凤凰通常是被描绘成相向的雌雄一对,象征着宇宙中阴阳二元性的相互依赖。

④ Down the ages, the Chinese dragon and the Chinese Phoenix embedded with people's blessing and hope are the symbols of blissful relations between husband and wife, and common metaphors of yin and yang.
在中国,自古以来,饱含人们美好祝愿的龙凤是夫妻幸福的象征,也是对阴阳的常见比喻。

Exercises

Task 1　Asking and Answering

Directions: *Read Text 1 carefully*, and answer the following questions.

(1) What marriage custom did Chinese follow in ancient times?
_____

(2) What do Three Letters refer to?
_____

(3) Why would the unmarried boy's parents locate a matchmaker?
_____

(4) Was a wedding day arranged according to the result of fortune-telling?
_____

(5) The daughter couldn't go back to her mother's home in the first year of marriage, could she?
_____

Task 2　Thinking and Judging

Directions: *Read Text 2 and judge whether the following statements are Yes (Y), No (N) or Not Given (NG)*.

Yes	if the statement agrees with the information given in the passage
No	if the statement contradicts the information given in the passage
Not Given	if the information is not given in the passage

(1) The Chinese dragon is often described as a composite of 9 beings. (   )

(2) As the Chinese dragon is an essential symbol of the spirit among Chinese, the Chinese dragon boat race and flying dragon kite in spring are also popular among the people. (   )

(3) Unlike the Chinese dragon, phoenix is a mythical creature. (   )

(4) The phoenix, often depicted in a pair with a male and a female facing each other, symbolizes everlasting love. (   )

(5) Our ancestors create many images to express their pursuit of a happy life. (   )

Task 3　Discussing and Writing

Directions: *Talk with your classmates about the traditional customs you know well, and share your personal attitude to Chinese traditional customs. Then write an essay about 150 words introducing one Chinese traditional custom.*

Task 4　Translating

Directions: *Complete the following sentences by translating the Chinese in brackets into English.*

(1) _____(他们已经感觉到了婚姻中潜在的问题), they are determined to have a talk.

(2) Today, _____(传统的婚姻习俗在某些地方已经恢复), attracting many prospective couples.

(3) _____(中国传统的吉祥物体现了深厚的民族思想) and they are outstanding cultural heritage with a glorious history.

(4) Our ancestors created many mascots _____(表达他们对幸福生活的追求), while modern Chinese mascots mainly play a communication role.

(5) Because the Chinese dragon _____(视为吉祥的象征), people have dragon dance to pray for good weather in order to achieve bumper harvest.

Section B　Listening and Speaking

Text 3　A Situational Dialogue on Fengshui

(J: *Jack, an American student learning Chinese in China*; *He Feng, a Chinese student*)

J: Recently I went to buy some books on Chinese culture; I noticed several people there were reading books on Fengshui. Would you please tell me something about it?

H: Fengshui is an ancient Chinese science originating from over 3,000 years ago. At beginning it was called Kan Yu①, denoting the monitoring of the activities of the forces between Heaven and Earth, but ever since the Qing Dynasty the term Fengshui has prevailed.

J: Really? What do Feng and Shui mean respectively?

H: Feng means wind and Shui means water. ①Fengshui is a traditional Chinese discipline which studies the way in which human beings co-exist in harmony with nature. It embodies a simple recognition of nature by our Chinese ancestors.

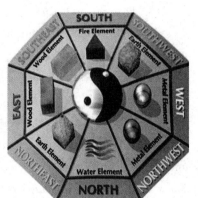

J: Sounds interesting! But how does Fengshui work?

H: ② Fengshui studies the energy circulation in nature as well as the effect of the living environment on people. The accumulated energy, or Qi, though invisible, is everywhere, affecting our existence with its power. On the one hand, it can be particularly positive and beneficial, bringing us good luck and wealth; on the other hand, not so positive, conveying hardships. When we are able to distinguish the energies in our environment by means of Fengshui, we gain the information enabling us to choose to live in good locations, compatible to our personal energy, and letting us receive the positive Qi from the environment. When we do not possess the Fengshui knowledge, it can easily happen that we — quite unintentionally — choose for ourselves a living environment bringing in unfavorable Qi, thus decreasing our chances to realize our potential and a quality life.

J: How can Fengshui produce such miracles? Are there any principles?

H: ③There are three principles of Fengshui: the unity of human beings with nature, the balance of Yin and Yang, and the attraction and repulsion of five elements — metal, wood, water, fire and earth. These principles are set up to help people pursue good fortune and avoid disasters, thus improving their living standard.

J: It is said that Fengshui is mainly used in community planning and architectural design.

H: Fengshui can also be used when there is a change in life goals and a change in family. Nowadays, Fengshui still plays an important role in people's lives. To improve their quality of life, many people decorate their houses according to Fengshui rules.

J: Is Fengshui based on a religion?

H: No. Fengshui is based on nature. Though there are many people who believe it's a kind of superstition, its wisdom can be made use of to enhance our lives.

---

① 风水古称堪舆术。堪者,天道也,舆者,地道也,就是研究天地之道的学说。相传风水的创始人是九天玄女,比较完善的风水学问起源于战国时代。风水的核心思想是人与大自然的和谐,是中国历史悠久的一门玄术。

J: If I want to get started with Fengshui, what do I need?

H: The desire to transform your life and the willingness to take action. Do you want to pursue some Fengshui studies of your own?

J: I'm absolutely interested in it, but first I must learn Chinese very hard and one day I'll read books on Fengshui by myself. (490 words)

(Based on http://www.afro-asia.info/destinations-China.php)

Difficult Sentences

① Fengshui is a traditional Chinese discipline which studies the way in which human beings co-exist in harmony with nature.
风水是中国的传统学科,研究人与自然和谐共存的方法。

② Fengshui studies the energy circulation in nature as well as the effect of the living environment on people.
风水研究的是能量在自然界的循环以及环境对人的影响。

③ There are three principles of Fengshui: the unity of human beings with nature, the balance of Yin and Yang, and the attraction and repulsion of five elements—metal, wood, water, fire and earth.
风水有三个原则:天人合一原则;阴阳平衡原则;金木水火土五行相生相克原则。

Text 4 An Introduction to Traditional Chinese Zodiac (生肖)

There are many legends and mythology related to Chinese zodiac and there are various versions and stories popular in different regions. Why were there twelve animals in the zodiac calendar and how did the order come from? Here are the most well-known stories as an important part of Chinese zodiacal culture.

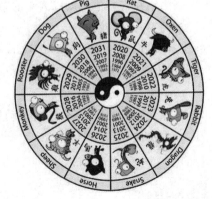

This is the most widespread legend about Chinese zodiac: The Jade Emperor①(The Emperor in Heaven in Chinese folklore) ordered that animals would be designated(选定) as calendar signs and the twelve that arrived first would be selected. ①The night before the event, the cat and his pal, the rat, agreed that the first to wake the following morning would wake the other. However, the rat broke his promise and arrived at the meeting first. On the way, he encountered the tiger,

---

① 玉皇大帝,也称为玉帝或玉皇。道教认为玉皇为众神之王,除统领天、地、人三界神灵之外,还管理宇宙万物的兴隆衰败、吉凶祸福。

the ox, the horse, and other animals that ran much faster. In order not to fall behind them, the rat jumped on the ox's back. ②As the ox was happy thinking that he would be the first sign of the years, the rat had already slid in front and became the first lucky animal of the Chinese zodiac. The ox was the second, then the tiger, the rabbit, the dragon, the snake, the horse, the sheep, the monkey, the rooster, the dog successively, and the lazy pig finished last. When the cat finally awoke and hurried to the meeting place, it was all over. According to the legend, this is why cats prey on rats.

③Based on this order of arrival, the Jade Emperor gave each animal a year of its own, bestowing(给与) the nature and characteristics of each animal on people born in the corresponding year.

About this simple story, there are different versions. Some say it was the Jade Emperor who intended to select twelve guards. Some say that the rat was too excited to recall his promise of waking the cat, and went directly to the gathering place. It is also said the animals were requested to have a swimming race; the cat and the rat were poor swimmers but quite intelligent, so they both agreed to hop on the back of the ox. Midway across the river, the rat pushed the cat into the water. (352 words)

(Based on http://www.travelchinaguide.com/intro/social_customs)

Difficult Sentences

① The night before the event, the cat and his pal, the rat, agreed that the first to wake the following morning would wake the other.

头天晚上,猫和他的好朋友老鼠约定先醒的一个要叫醒另外一个。

② As the ox was happy thinking that he would be the first sign of the years, the rat had already slid in front, and became the first lucky animal of the Chinese zodiac,

当牛正在窃喜他可以成为年的第一个标志时,老鼠已经跳到了他的前面幸运地成为了生肖的第一个动物。

③ Based on this order of arrival, the Jade Emperor gave each animal a year of its own, bestowing(给予) the nature and characteristics of each animal on people born in the corresponding year.

按照到达的顺序,玉帝按每个动物的名字来命名年,并给予在相应的年份出生的人以相应的特性。

Exercises

Task 1 Listening and Answering

Directions: *Listen to the dialogue twice and then answer the following questions according to the dialogue.*

Unit 6
Traditional Customs

(1) When did Fengshui originate?

(2) What does Fengshui study?

(3) Are there any principles of Fengshui?

(4) Why are these three principles set up?

(5) What is Fengshui based on? A religion?

Task 2 Listening and Speaking

Directions: *Listen to the introduction about traditional Chinese zodiac and retell it briefly; then, share other stories about traditional Chinese zodiac with your classmates.*

Task 3 Vocabulary Building

Directions: *Complete the following sentences with the words taken from the above two listening materials. Change the forms if necessary.*

| encounter | correspond | intend | intelligent | recognition |
| harmony | analyze | ensure | pursue | transform |

(1) The architecture is _____ and no building is over five or six floors high.

(2) In the last _____, the responsibility for this failure must lie with the husband.

(3) The money is _____ for the wedding ceremony.

(4) He is an outstanding player who doesn't get the _____ he deserves.

(5) The divorced couple were angry when they _____, but they parted with smile.

(6) With the improving economic situation, people are able to _____ better living conditions.

(7) These principles are fundamental to _____ that we can exist in harmony with the surroundings.

(8) The Web is certainly a _____ technology, just as TV and radio and newspapers once were.

(9) People born in the _____ year are bestowed with the characteristics of 12 animals respectively.

(10) They are incapable of thinking _____ about politics.

Translation Practice

Directions: *Translate the following passages into English.*

(1) 中国龙是吉祥的生灵，象征着力量、智慧和好运。龙被尊崇为雨神，能掌握风和水。在干旱或水灾发生时，人们会去当地的龙王庙烧香祈求情况的好转。龙对雨水和海浪的控制也和其在12生肖中的地位密切相关。这12种动物的顺序是按各自最活跃的时间点确定的。龙对应于7点至9点，此时天空会雾气蒙蒙，龙就能腾云驾雾。

(2) 风水，古时也被称为堪舆，是中国传统文化的重要组成部分。它依据诸如道家和《易经》等中国古代哲学学说，强调了人与环境的和谐共存。事实上，古时它是被广泛应用于东方建筑的一种古老艺术。中国的许多著名的文化名胜，包括北京的故宫，都是按照风水原则设计的。风水学对中国社会产生了深远的影响并为大众所接受。

Words and Expressions Related to Traditional Customs
中国古代习俗相关词汇与表达方式

stay up late or all night on New Year's Eve	守岁	Jade Emperor	玉皇大帝
Spring Festival couplets	春联	imperial guardian lions	守门石狮
door-god	门神	flying kites	放风筝
pay a new year call	拜年	dragon dance	舞龙
gift money for a new year	压岁钱	walking on stilts	踩高跷
cheongsam	旗袍	dragon-boat racing	赛龙舟
hanging the Chinese mugwort leaf	挂艾叶	setting off fireworks	放鞭炮
feet-binding	裹脚	watching lanterns	观灯
Chinese lunar calendar	农历	guessing / solving lantern riddles	猜灯谜
eating Zongzi	吃粽子	lion dance	舞狮
twenty-four solar terms	二十四节气	tomb sweeping	扫墓
paper resembling money	纸钱	Laba Festival	腊八
Laba rice porridge	腊八粥	eight characters	生辰八字
Heavenly Stem	天干	Earthly Branch	地支
fortune-telling	算命	the Kitchen God Festival	小年

Unit 6
Traditional Customs

Key to Unit 6 Exercises

Before You Start

1. Chinese culture is rich in traditional customs, such as customs of marriage and its preparation, funeral and the wake, birthday and naming, speech and greeting conventions, dining and celebrating festivals, and even colours and numbers have their specific meanings in traditional Chinese culture.

2. Traditional customs are quite different from superstitions. Just take some customs and superstitions that many Chinese adhere to during the New Year for example. Shooting off firecrackers on Chinese New Year's Eve is the traditional Chinese way of sending out the old year and welcoming the new. But on the stroke of midnight, every door and every window in the house have to be opened to allow the old year to go out as one of the Chinese superstitions goes. It is another superstitious belief of the Chinese that if one has a dream of teeth or snow, it indicates that his parents are dead or drying.

Section A Reading and Writing

Exercises

Task 1 **Asking and Answering**

(1) Three Letters and Six Etiquettes.

(2) Three Letters include Betrothal Letter, Gift Letter and Wedding Letter.

(3) Because a matchmaker could assuage the conflict of interests and general embarrassments when discussing the possibility of marriage on the part of two families largely unknown to each other.

(4) No, it was arranged according to Chinese Tung Shing.

(5) Yes, the daughter could go back at anytime.

Task 2 **Thinking and Judging**

(1) Y (2) NG (3) N (4) Y (5) Y

Task 3 **Discussing and Writing**

Sample1: An Introduction to Benming Nian (Year of Birth)

The animal year when a person was born is called his/her Benming Nian (year of birth). The distinctive zodiacal way of calculating years based on the lunar calendar decides that every once in every twelve year cycle people will meet their birth sign.

It is said that in one's year of birth, he will offend "taisui", a mysterious power that could control people's fortune. The best way to avoid miserable events is to wear red clothes or a red waistband especially during the Spring Festival. This may be due to the people's special affection for red since redness is the token of festivities, success and exorcism.

Like most Chinese customs, some pay no attention to it while others adhere to it. My friend told me his parents did believe in this and made him wear red underwears during his Benming Nian. For me, a change to one's fate to ensure good fortune requires both effort and a firm belief. (159 words)

Sample 2: An Introduction to the Qingming Festival

The Qingming Festival is one of the 24 seasonal division points in China. After it, the temperature will rise up and rainfall increases. It is not only a seasonal point to guide farm work, but a festival of commemoration.

The Qingming Festival sees a combination of sadness and happiness. People at this time offer sacrifices to their ancestors and sweep the tombs of the deceased. Also, they will not cook on this day and only cold food is served. The Hanshi Festival was usually one day before the Qingming Festival; then, they were later combined.

In contrast to the sadness of the tomb sweepers, people also enjoy hope of spring on this day. The Qingming Festival is a time when the sun shines brightly, so is a time to plant trees, for the survival rate of saplings is high and trees grow fast later. In the past, the Qingming Festival was also called "Arbor Day". (158 words)

Task 4 Translating

(1) Having noticed the potential problem in their marriage

(2) traditional marriage customs have been revived in some places

(3) Traditional Chinese mascots embody profound national ideas

(4) to express their pursuit of a happy life

(5) is looked upon as the symbol of good fortune

Section B Listening and Speaking

Task 1 Listening and Answering

(1) It originated from over 3,000 years ago

(2) It studies human beings co-existing in harmony with nature/the energy circulation in nature as well as the effect of the living environment on people.

(3) Yes, there are three principles of Fengshui: (The unity of human beings with nature, the balance of Yin and Yang, and the attraction and repulsion of five elements — metal, wood, water, fire and earth.)

(4) To help people pursue good fortune and avoid disaster

(5) Fengshui is based on nature.

Task 3 Vocabulary Building

(1) harmonious   (2) analysis   (3) intended   (4) recognition

(5) encountered   (6) pursue   (7) ensure   (8) transformative
(9) corresponding   (10) intelligently

参考译文

(1) The Chinese dragon is an auspicious(吉祥的) creature, symbolizing strength, wisdom and good luck. The dragon was worshiped as the God of Rain with power over the elements of wind and water. In times of drought or flooding, locals would visit a dragon-king temple and burn incense(香) to pray for more favorable conditions. The dragon's power to control rain and waves is also closely related to its rank in the 12 zodiac animals. The sequence of the 12 animals is determined by the time of day when each animal is most active. The dragon corresponds to 7 a.m. to 9 a.m., when it is most likely to be foggy, allowing the dragon to ride atop clouds and mist.

(2) Fengshui, also called Kan Yu in ancient times, is an important part of traditional Chinese culture. Based on ancient Chinese philosophies, including Taoism and the *I Ching*, Fengshui emphasizes the harmonious coexistence(共存) of humans and their environment. In fact, it was an ancient art widely used in orient(东方的) buildings in olden times. Many of China's well-known cultural attractions, including the Forbidden City in Beijing, were designed in Fengshui principles. Fengshui has a profound effect on Chinese society and is widely embraced by the public.

Unit 7

Beijing in History

导读

本单元是对古都北京的简要介绍,旨在使学生对北京城的基本概貌、历史变迁、城市结构、建筑风格等有所了解,掌握相关的英文表达方式,在今后对外交流中能够用规范、流畅的语言进行有关首都北京的译介,让这座古都穿越历史、走向世界。

Before You Start

While you are preparing for this unit, think about the following questions:
1. How many names did Beijing have in history? What are they?
2. What do you know about the gates of the inner city of Beijing?
3. Where do you prefer to live, in an apartment or a Siheyuan? Why?

Section A Reading and Writing

Text 1 A Brief History of Beijing

Beijing is one of the four ancient cities of China (together with Xi'an, Luoyang, Nanjing), whose origins can be traced back to over 2,000 years ago. During the Western Zhou Dynasty (11th century BC—771 BC), the emperor gave the feudal lords under his rule plots of land, or feod (封地;采邑), one of which was called "Ji City"(蓟城). It was the capital of the kingdom "Ji" at that time. This city was the earliest in Beijing history. By the time of the Eastern Zhou Period (476 BC—221 BC), the kingdom Ji was replaced by the kingdom "Yan". However, Ji City was still the capital city.

Unit 7

Beijing in History

Since 221 BC Beijing has played an important role in the northern part of China. During Sui (581 to 618) and Tang (618 to 907) Dynasties, Beijing, which was called "Zhuo"(涿) and "You"(幽) respectively, was not only a strategic military place but also the major trade center.

In 938, Beijing was conquered by the Khitans① (Qidan) and declared one of the two capitals of the Liao Dynasty (907—1125). At that time the city, located in the southern part of their kingdom, was named Nanjing.

In 1125, the Jurchen②(northern nomadic tribe) of the Jin Dynasty conquered the Liao and renamed the city Yanjing(燕京). In 1153, Jin Emperor Wanyan Liang③ moved his capital from Shangjing(上京)(near present-day Harbin) to Beijing, calling it Zhongdu(中都). The golden Imperial Palace was established in Zhongdu at that time, which was the first time in Beijing history that the city became a truly significant capital.

Eventually, Genghis Khan's④ Mongolian army conquered the Jin and utterly destroyed the city in 1215. In 1267 Kublai Khan⑤ ordered the construction of his new capital in the northeast suburbs of Zhongdu at the site of present-day Beijing. Four years later in 1271, Kublai Khan established the Yuan Dynasty with Yuan Dadu(元大都) (currently Beijing) as the capital. ①When the Mongols finally eliminated the Southern Song and unified China, Dadu became the political center of the country for the first time in history.

The construction of Dadu ended in 1293. ②It consisted of three main projects—the imperial palaces, the city walls and moats(护城河), and the canal. The city was rectangular with regular chessboard pattern whose layout(布局) was the result of uniform planning. Dadu enjoyed great fame in the 13th century world. The Italian traveler Marco Polo wrote in his travel notes that he considered it to be the "incommensurable city even in the world".

In 1368, Ming troops captured Dadu and the city was renamed Beiping. However Zhu Yuanzhang, the founder of the Ming Dynasty (1368—1644) made Nanjing his first capital.

---

① 契丹：中国北方草原的游牧民族。唐代末年建立了强大的地方政权,唐灭亡的907年建立契丹国,后改称辽,统治中国北方。元朝之后,这一民族逐渐销声匿迹。

② 女真：中国古代生活于东北地区的古老民族,现今满族、赫哲族、鄂伦春族等的前身。12世纪前期建立了金朝,统治中国北方一百多年之久。直至13世纪被蒙古人所灭。17世纪初建州女真部逐渐强大,其首领努尔哈赤统一了女真诸部,1616年建立后金政权,至1636年,皇太极改女真族号为满洲,女真一词就此停止使用。

③ 海陵王完颜亮(1122—1161)为金朝第四任皇帝,1149年即位,在位12年。在熙宗改革的基础上,进一步进行改革,加强中央集权;迁都燕京加速汉化。但海陵王荒淫无度,1161年,被部将所杀,时年40岁。

④ 成吉思汗,元太祖,名铁木真(1162—1227)。公元1206年,被推举为蒙古帝国大汗(后被尊为元朝开国皇帝),统一蒙古各部落,取得了"成吉思汗"的名称("最高统治者")。在位期间,多次发动征服战争,攻金灭夏,征服地域西达黑海海滨,东括几乎整个东亚,建立了世界史上著名的横跨欧亚两洲的大帝国。

⑤ 忽必烈(1215—1294),即元世祖,元朝创建者,成吉思汗之孙。1260年,忽必烈成为蒙古帝国大汗。1271年正式建国号为"大元"(1271—1368),定都大都,也就是今天的北京。自此以后,明、清两代,北京一直是国家的首都。公元1279年,实现了中国南北大统一。

In 1403, Zhu Di, the fourth son of Zhu Yuanzhang captured the throne and became the third emperor of the Ming Dynasty. In 1421 he formally transferred the capital from Nanjing to Beiping and, for the first time, named the city Beijing. It was during this period that the present grid(网格) pattern of the central city was established, arranged around a north-south axis centering on the Imperial Palace. ③ The city's design followed the traditional architectural principles of Fengshui to achieve maximum harmony between the human and natural world.

In 1644, the Manchus(满族人) overthrew the declining Ming Dynasty and established China's last imperial line, the Qing Dynasty. During this era, the Qing largely retained the physical arrangement of Beijing inside the city walls. ④ Each of the Eight Manchu Banners was assigned to guard and live near the eight gates of the Inner City. Outside the city, the Qing Court seized large tracts of land for Manchu noble estates. ⑤Northwest of the city, Qing emperors built several large palatial gardens, including Qingyiyuan(清漪园,后改名为颐和园) and Yuanmingyuan, which were ransacked and razed by invading Western powers at the end of the Qing Dynasty.

It was until October 1st, 1949 that the People's Republic of China was founded. As the capital city of the prosperous new country, Beijing has flared into importance in Asia, changing with each passing day. (672 words)

(Based on http://history.cultural-china.com/en/34 History 12117.html)

Difficult Sentences

① When the Mongols finally eliminated the Southern Song and unified China, Dadu became the political center of the country for the first time in history.
当蒙古人最后灭掉南宋统一中国的时候,大都在历史上第一次成为国家的政治中心。

② It consisted of three main projects— the imperial palaces, the city walls and moats(护城河), and the canal. The city was rectangular with regular chessboard pattern whose layout was the result of uniform planning.
元大都包括三个主要的工程:皇宫、城墙及护城河、运河。整个城市是一座呈规则棋盘格局的长方形城池,其布局是统一规划的结果。

③ The city's design followed the traditional architectural principles of Fengshui to achieve maximum harmony between the human and natural world.
城市的设计沿袭了传统建筑的风水原则,以期实现人与自然的最大和谐。

④ Each of the Eight Manchu Banners was assigned to guard and live near the eight gates of the Inner City.
满族八旗中的每一旗分别被指派去保卫内城的八个城门,并驻守在城门附近。

⑤ Northwest of the city, Qing emperors built several large palatial gardens, including Qingyiyuan and Yuanmingyuan, which were ransacked and razed by invading Western

Unit 7
Beijing in History

powers at the end of the Qing Dynasty.

清朝皇帝在北京城的西北部建造了几个富丽堂皇的大花园,其中就有清漪园和圆明园。清朝末年,西方列强入侵,圆明园惨遭洗劫破坏。

Text 2 Walls and Gates of Beijing

As an ancient capital of China, the history of Beijing's city wall probably dates back to the later period of the Shang Dynasty (16th—17th century BC). Early in 1045 B.C., Yan built up the city wall (now located in the northwest of Beijing). ① From then on, the history of Beijing's city wall culture was initiated and was hereafter also subject to vicissitudes(变迁兴衰) and new development along with the historical evolution.

The well-founded ancient city wall in Beijing was built in Zhongdu, the capital city of the Jin Dynasty (265—420), which was the rudiment of the present Beijing. Mongol rulers of the Yuan Dynasty destroyed the Jin capital. ② In 1267 Yuan rulers abandoned the site of the former Jin capital and constructed a new city known as Dadu, centered in the Jin emperor's auxiliary (附属的) palaces. This was the embryonic(初期的) form of present-day Beijing.

Urn-shaped city

In 1368, Zhu Yuanzhang, the first Ming emperor, attacked and captured the Yuan capital Dadu and established his new capital at Nanjing. His son Zhu Di renamed Beiping Beijing in 1403, and in 1421 officially made it the capital of China.

During the Ming Dynasty, Beijing set up its own guard system to defend itself. Because of the great threat of the Mongolian tribes, Beijing's City Wall and Gates were well constructed. Qing extended Ming's Wall with urn-shaped city(瓮城) around each Gate. The system of Beijing's old town comprises 4 levels: Outer City, Inner City, Imperial City, and Forbidden City.

西直门城楼、箭楼、瓮城

The inner city has nine city gates, (Xuanwu Gate, Fucheng Gate, Xizhi Gate, Desheng Gate, Anding Gate, Dongzhi Gate, Chaoyang Gate, Chongwen Gate and Zhengyang Gate①), whereas the outer city has seven city gates (Dongbian Gate, Guangqu Gate, Zuo'an Gate, Yongding Gate, You'an Gate and Guang'an Gate).

Each of the Gates consists of a Gate, a Fort Tower(箭楼), and an urn-shaped city.

---

① 正阳门:俗称前门,位于北京城南北中轴线上,在天安门广场南缘,前门大街北端,始建于明永乐十七年,原名丽正门,后改称正阳门。

③There are no direct entrances to the Gate in the Inner City, so people have to walk around the Fort Tower to the side door to enter the urn-shaped city, and then go in through the Gate (Zhengyang Gate is the only exception).

Each city gate has a different function. For instance, Chaoyang Gate is used for grain to pass through; Chongwen Gate is for wine; Xuanwu Gate is for the prisoner van; Fucheng Gate is for coal and so on. The main function of the city wall is military defense. In traditional times, the imperial military would march out of Beijing through Desheng Gate, and return through Anding Gate, the Gate of Peace and Stability.

There are four City Gates in the Imperial City(皇城), the well known Tian'an Gate is one of them. The other three are: Di'an Gate, Xi'an Gate, Dong'an Gate. The Forbidden City also has four gates: Wu Gate, Shenwu Gate, Xihua Gate, and Donghua Gate.

As for the 16 city gates in Inner City and Outer City, they are constructed symmetrically(对称地) because of an axis in Beijing. Generally speaking, Inner City Gates are much larger than Outer City's as far as the construction style is concerned. The largest gate is Zhengyang Gate, which is 25 meters high, and is still standing today. The smallest is Xibian Gate, which is only 11.2 meters high and 11.5 meters wide.

Besides, Fuxing Gate and Jianguo Gate are not real "Gates"; they were just opened breaches(豁口) on the wall. They were "built" during Japaneses invasion. Heping Gate and a less famous Shuiguan Gate were opened by foreign forces in 1900. Obviously, they are not "Gates" at all.

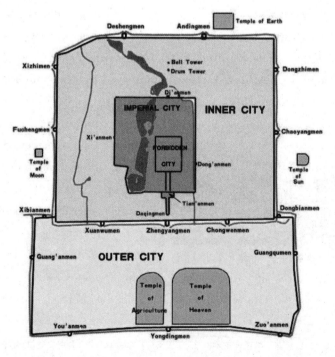

Map of Beijing City Wall

Beijing's City Wall and Gates have been torn down in the process of urban construction. But fortunately, there are some relics standing today. The government realized the importance of the reconstruction of some of the Gates, so that's why Yongding Gate was reconstructed in the year 2005. (624 words)

(Based on: http://www.chinahistoryforum.com/index.php?/topic/16462-what-is-left-of-beijing's-city-walls)

Difficult Sentences

① From then on, the history of Beijing's city wall culture was initiated and was hereafter also subject to vicissitudes(变迁兴衰) and new development along with the historical evolution.

从那时起,北京城墙文化的历史拉开序幕,此后随着历史的演变也经历了变迁兴衰和新的发展。

② In 1267 Yuan rulers abandoned the site of the former Jin capital and constructed a new city known as Dadu, centered in the Jin emperor's auxiliary palaces.

1267年元朝统治者放弃了前金国都城遗址,以金国皇帝的偏殿为中心建成一座新城名为大都。

③ There are no direct entrances to the Gate in the Inner City, so people had to walk around the Fort Tower to the side door to enter the urn-shaped city, and then go in through the Gate (Zhengyang Gate is the only exception).

内城的城门没有直接的入口,所以人们必须绕过箭楼从侧门进入瓮城,然后才能穿过城门进入城内(正阳门是唯一的例外)。

Exercises

Task 1 Skimming and Scanning

Directions: *In this part, you will have 10 minutes to go over Text 1 quickly, then answer the following questions.*

For questions 1—7, mark

Y (for YES) if the statement agrees with the information given in the passage;

N (for NO) if the statement contradicts the information given in the passage;

NG (for NOT GIVEN) if the information is not given in the passage.

For questions 8—10, *complete the sentences with the information given in the passage.*

(   ) (1) During the Sui and Tang Dynasties, Beijing was called "Zhuo".

(   ) (2) In 938, Beijing was conquered by the Khitans (Qidan) and became the only capital of the Liao Dynasty.

(   ) (3) The Jurchen of the Jin Dynasty conquered the Liao and renamed the city

Nanjing.

（　　）(4) The golden Imperial Palace built in Zhongdu demonstrated that for the first time in Beijing history the city became a truly significant capital.

（　　）(5) Genghis Khan's Mongolian army conquered the Liao and did some damage to the city in 1215.

（　　）(6) When the Southern Song was eliminated and China was unified, Dadu became the political, economic and cultural center of the country for the first time in history.

（　　）(7) Ming troops captured Dadu and the city was renamed Beijing.

(8) The city's design followed the traditional architectural principles of Fengshui to _____.

(9) The Manchus overthrew the declining Ming Dynasty and established _____.

(10) Each of the Eight Manchu Banners was assigned to guard and _____.

Task 2　Thinking and Writing

Directions: *Qianmen is a must-see scenic spot in China. Please write an essay on Qianmen according to the outline below:*

(1) *The brief history of Qianmen*

(2) *The present situation of Qianmen*

(3) *The geographical significance of Qianmen*

Task 3　Research and Development

Directions: *Beijing, one of the ancient cities of China, has a lot of places of interest which are worth a visit. Please design a One-day tour for your classmates.*

Section B　Listening and Speaking

Text 3　Situational Dialogue: About the Forbidden City

(D: David, an American student learning Chinese in China. Z: Zhao Li, a Chinese student.)

D: Do you think the Forbidden City is well worth a visit?

Z: Of course! I highly recommend it.

D: Would you like to tell me something about the Forbidden City?

Z: Certainly.

D: That is very kind of you. When was the Forbidden City built?

Unit 7 Beijing in History

Z: It was built between 1406 and 1420 during the Ming Dynasty, being the imperial home of 24 emperors of the Ming and Qing Dynasties.

D: Wow, it has such a long history. Why was it built?

Z: It was built as a means of protection for Chinese emperors and their family.

D: Oh, I see. As the largest and most well-preserved imperial palace extant(现存的) in China, it is said to have 9,999.5 rooms. Is that true?

Z: No, the 9,999 rooms and a half is just a myth. Only the heavenly emperor could be so well qualified to have entire 10,000 rooms. The emperor declared himself the son of the heavenly emperor, so his palace couldn't be larger than his father's. Therefore, it had a half room less when it was built. However, in ancient Chinese architecture, one room refers to a square space among four pillars in a hall. Therefore, it is impossible to have a half room among four pillars. By the last count, including big and small palaces, halls, towers, pavilions, belvederes(观景楼), there are 8,707 rooms.

D: What a spacious palace! I have heard that many gates inside the imperial city, especially the huge red gates of the major structures, are decorated with gilded doornails (门钉) counted by 9. Would you please tell me the reason?

Z: Of course. ①The reason is that "9" was regarded as the biggest number in ancient China and it was used to imply the emperor, resembling the imperial power in a symbolic sense.

D: That is quite interesting. By the way, although I haven't visited the Forbidden City in person, I have seen the pictures of it. I think its layout and architecture are quite unique.

Z: Absolutely correct. ② The general layout of the Forbidden City is like this: a number of axes are used to deploy such a large number of buildings, and all these buildings are developed in the form of courtyard. In each courtyard there are buildings in groups. Some buildings are subordinate to others, and some buildings are dominated by others. ③ By using this kind of architectural language, the hierarchy and order of feudal society and the feudal set of rituals are successfully expressed.

D: Oh, that is so amazing! Thank you for providing me so many details. Would you like to accompany me to visit it at your convenience?

Z: No problem!

D: It is so nice of you. I am afraid it is time for my class. I've got to go. I will call you later. See you!

Z: See you! (488 words)

(Based on http://www.travelchinaguide.com/attraction/beijing/forbidden-city/faq.htm)

Difficult Sentences

① The reason is that "9" was regarded as the biggest number in ancient China and it was used to imply the emperor, resembling the imperial power in a symbolic sense.

因为在古代中国"九"被看做是最大的数字,在象征意义上与皇权类似,所以被用来暗指皇帝。

② The general layout of the Forbidden City is like this: a number of axes are used to deploy such a large number of buildings, and all these buildings are developed in the form of courtyard.
紫禁城的总体布局是这样的:数量众多的建筑物沿着多条轴线分布,并且所有这些建筑物都建成庭院的格局。

③ By using this kind of architectural language, the hierarchy and order of feudal society and the feudal set of rituals are successfully expressed.
通过使用这种建筑语言,封建社会的等级秩序和封建礼教得到了成功的表达。

Text 4　A Tour guide to Beijing's Hutong and Siheyuan

◆ **Hutong**

Hutongs are a type of narrow streets or alleys, most commonly associated with Beijing, China. ① Historically, a hutong was also once used as the lowest level of administrative geographical divisions within a city in ancient China.

Qianjing Hutong, Beijing

"Hutong" is not originally a Chinese word, but a word taken from Mongolian, which means "water well". Mongolian people lived a nomadic life in northern grassland and often gathered to live near water sources. So the original meaning of Hutong should be "a place where people gather and live".

Another explanation says that during the Yuan Dynasty around the 13th century, residential areas in the city were divided into many divisions. Between the smaller divisions were passageways for people to travel through, and those passageways also functioned as isolation belts against fire risks. In Mongolian language, passageways of this kind were called Hutong.

No matter what Hutong exactly means, one thing is for certain that Hutongs first appeared in Beijing during the Yuan Dynasty and were preserved until now. ② In contrast to the court life and elite culture represented by the Forbidden City, the Summer Palace, and the Temple of Heaven, the hutongs represent the culture and lifestyle of traditional Beijing citizens, the common people. As a result, hutong can be seen as a continuation of Beiing's history and culture.

Unit 7
Beijing in History

◆ **Siheyuan**

A Siheyuan is a traditional unique folk house in the hutongs. It dated from the Ming Dynasty. "Si" means "Four", which here refers to the four sides: east, west, north and south. "He" refers to the surrounding, meaning the four sides circled into a square. ③Due to its special layout, it is compared to a box with a garden in the center. There is only one gate leading to a hutong, so when the gate is closed the courtyard loses touch with the outside world. Therefore family members can fully enjoy tranquility and share the happiness of a peaceful family union.

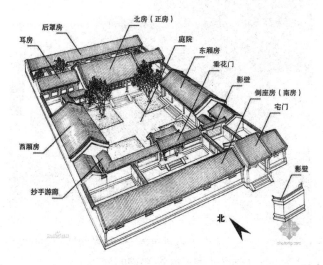

The buildings of a Siheyuan are normally positioned along the north-south and east-west axes. The building positioned to the north and facing the south is considered the main house (正房). The buildings adjoining the main house and facing east and west are called side houses (厢房). ④ The northern, eastern and western buildings are connected by beautifully decorated pathways (游廊), serving as shelters from the sunshine during the day and providing a cool place to appreciate the view of the courtyard at night. The building that faces north is known as the opposite house (倒座房). ⑤Behind the northern building, there would often be a separate backside building (后罩房) for unmarried daughters and female servants. As unmarried girls were not allowed direct exposure to the public, they occupied the most secluded building in the Siheyuan. It is the only place where two-story buildings are allowed to be constructed for the traditional Siheyuan.

⑥The courtyard dwellings are built according to the traditional concepts of the five elements that are believed to compose the universe, and the eight diagrams of divination for the consideration of the "fengshui". The entrance gate, usually painted vermilion(朱红色的) and with copper door knockers(门环) on it, is usually at the southeastern corner which is the "wind" corner, and the main house is built on the north side which is believed to belong to "water", an element to prevent fire. Normally, there is a screen wall called

Yingbi(影壁) inside the gate for privacy; superstition holds that it also protects the house from evil spirits. A pair of stone lions are often placed outside the gate.

A Siheyuan offers space, comfort, quiet and privacy, reflecting the ritualistic and traditional ideas of China, and containing rich cultural connotations. Because of the historic and cultural value of Siheyuan, it will certainly be worthy of being well protected. (637 words)

(Based on http://en.wikipedia.org/wiki/Hutong

http://www.travelchinaguide.com/cityguides/beijing/hutong/yard.htm)

The entrance gate and screen wall of Mei Lanfang Museum, a typical Beijing Siheyuan

Difficult Sentences

① Historically, a hutong was also once used as the lowest level of administrative geographical divisions within a city in ancient China.
从历史上看,胡同还曾经被用来作为中国古代城市行政区划的最低划分级别。

② In contrast to the court life and elite culture represented by the Forbidden City, the Summer Palace, and the Temple of Heaven, the hutongs represent the culture and lifestyle of traditional Beijing citizens, the common people.
与紫禁城、颐和园、天坛所象征的宫廷生活和精英文化相比,胡同则代表了老北京市民,即普通人的文化和生活方式。

③ Due to its special layout, it is compared to a box with a garden in the center.
由于其特殊的布局,四合院被比喻成一个中心为花园的盒状结构。

④ The northern, eastern and western buildings are connected by beautifully decorated pathways(游廊), serving as shelters from the sunshine during the day and providing a cool place to appreciate the view of the courtyard at night.
装饰精美的游廊连接了北部、东部和西部的建筑物,白天遮阳,晚上则提供了一个欣赏庭院景致的清凉场所。

Unit 7
Beijing in History

⑤ Behind the northern building, there would often be a separate backside building (后罩房) for unmarried daughters and female servants, as unmarried girls were not allowed direct exposure to the public, they occupied the most secluded building in the Siheyuan.
正房后面通常建有一后罩房,为未婚女儿和女佣等女眷的居住之地;未婚小姐不允许直接在公众面前露面,所以她们住在四合院最僻静的房间。

⑥ The courtyard dwellings are built according to the traditional concepts of the five elements that are believed to compose the universe, and the eight diagrams of divination for the consideration of the "fengshui".
四合院是依据"五行"和"八卦"的传统观念建造的。人们认为"五行"是构成宇宙的要素,而占卜的八卦图则是出于"风水"的考虑。

Exercises

Task 1 Listening and Speaking

Directions: *Listen to the dialogue carefully. Discuss with your classmates about the Forbidden City and answer the following questions.*

1. When was the Forbidden City built?
2. How many emperors lived in the Forbidden City in the history?
3. Why was the Forbidden City built?
4. Is it true that there are 9,999.5 rooms in the Forbidden City?
5. Why are many gates inside the imperial city decorated with gilded doornails counted by 9?

Task 2 Vocabulary Building

Directions: *Complete the following sentences with the words listed below. Change the forms if necessary.*

| associate | administrate | expose | origin | explain |
| ritual | resident | private | history | oppose |

(1) "Hutong" is _____ a word taken from Mongolian, which means "water well".

(2) Do you think it is true that Hutongs, a type of narrow streets or alleys, are most commonly _____ with Beijing, China?

(3) I believe a hutong was once used as the lowest level of _____ geographical divisions within a city in ancient China.

(4) Can you tell us the accurate _____ of the origin of the word "Hutong" in Chinese?

(5) During the Yuan Dynasty _____ areas in the city were divided into many divisions.

（6）The building that faces north is known as the _____ house.

（7）In the old society of China, unmarried girls were not allowed direct _____ to the public.

（8）Normally, Yingbi(影壁), a screen wall, is constructed inside the gate of Siheyuan for _____.

（9）A Siheyuan reflects the _____ and traditional ideas of China.

（10）The Siheyuan should be well protected because of the _____ and cultural value.

Translation Practice

Directions: *Translate the following passages into English.*

（1）首都北京是中华人民共和国政治、文化和行政管理的中心，是一个新旧交融、魅力无限的大都市(metropolis)。北京作为人类居住地的历史已超过了3000多年。作为世界上少数未傍主要河道而建的内陆首都之一，北京将自己长期显赫的历史归功于战略性的地理位置。北京雄踞于华北平原(the North China Plain)的最北部；西北部是山西省和内蒙古大草原(the Inner Mongolian Steppe)，东向是渤海(the Bohai Sea)。

（2）胡同即狭窄的街道或巷子，在中国北方的城市很常见，其中又以北京的胡同最为著名。在北京，很多街区是这样形成的：四合院(Chinese quadrangle)彼此相连形成胡同，进而胡同彼此相连形成街区。胡同是北京文化要素的代表。由于北京悠久的历史和六朝古都的地位，几乎每个胡同都有其轶事趣闻(anecdotes)，一些胡同甚至还与历史事件紧密相关。与紫禁城、颐和园和天坛所代表的宫廷生活和精英文化(elite culture)相比，胡同反映了北京的平民文化。

Words and Expressions Related to the Historical City—Beijing
北京城历史相关词汇与表达方式

Ji City	蓟城
Yanjing	燕京
Zhongdu	中都
Genghis Khan	成吉思汗
Khitan	契丹
moat	护城河
chessboard pattern	棋盘格局
Marco Polo	马可·波罗

Unit 7
Beijing in History

vicissitude	变迁兴衰
urn-shaped city	瓮城
Fort Tower	箭楼
breaches on the wall	城墙的豁口
anecdote	轶事
Celestial Emperor / Jade Emperor	玉皇大帝
for the consideration of the "fengshui"	出于风水的考虑
the hierarchy and order of feudal society	封建社会的等级秩序
main house	正房
side house	厢房
pathway	廊
the opposite house	倒座房
backside building	后罩房
Yingbi	影壁
containing rich cultural connotations	包含丰富的文化内涵

Key to Unit 7 Exercises

Before You Start

1. The city has held many other names, some directly, some as a result of various territories it administered.

• Ji and Jicheng: The first major known settlement was the eponymous capital of the ancient Ji (蓟) state between the 11th and 7th centuries BC. The settlement was also known as Jicheng (蓟城). It was located in the current city's Guang'anmen neighborhood, south of the modern Beijing West Railway Station.

• Yan and Yanjing: Ji was conquered by Yan around the 7th century BC and was its conqueror's new capital with its name changed as Yan (燕) and Yanjing (燕京). The name was employed in the titles of An Lushan (as Emperor of Yan), Liu Rengong (as King of Yan), and the Princes of Yan. The Khitans (the 10th—12th century) of Liao Dynasty fully restored the name Yanjing and it remains a common informal name for Beijing.

• Guangyang: Upon its conquest by Qin, Ji was made the capital of the Guangyang Commandery (广阳郡).

• Fanyang and Yuyang: During the Han Dynasty, the commandery was renamed Yuyang (渔阳郡) and the city itself renamed Fanyang (范阳).

- Jixian: From the 1ˢᵗ century BC until at least the 4th century AD, in Western Jin Dynasty, Jixian (蓟县) served as the capital of Youzhou province.
- Youzhou: In the Tang Dynasty, the city generally employed Youzhou (幽州) as its name. During the Tianbao Era of Emperor Xuanzong, however, the name Fanyang was restored as its own commandery.
- Nanjing: In the 10th and 12th centuries, the northerly Liao Dynasty restored the name Yanjing. They also (ironically) knew the city as Nanjing (南京) as it was the southernmost of their secondary capitals.
- Zhongdu: During the 12th century, the Later Jin Dynasty, it was known as Zhongdu (中都, "Central Capital").
- Khanbaliq: The Mongolian Yuan Dynasty originally restored the name Yanjing before constructing a new capital adjacent to the former settlement. This settlement was called Dadu (大都) in Chinese and Daidu in Mongolian. (As Khanbaliq, it was noted as Cambuluc by Marco Polo.) This city gradually absorbed the former settlements around the area.
- Beiping: In the Ming Dynasty, the city itself was initially known as Beiping (北平).
- Shuntian and Beizhili: When the usurping Yongle Emperor established his base of Beiping as a secondary capital in 1403, he renamed the town Shuntian (顺天) and the region Beizhili (北直隶) to mimic the names of Yingtian (modern Nanjing).
- Jingshi and Beijing: When the palace was finally completed in 1421, the Yongle Emperor moved the majority of his court north. The name Jingshi (京师) ceased to be used for Yingtian and was now employed for Shuntian. The area around Yingtian became known as Nanjing while Beijing was used to describe the area directly administered by the capital (generally modern Hebei).
- Beiping (北平), was restored as the name in 1928 by the Republic of China following its reconquest of Beijing from the warlords during the Northern Expedition. The naming was again reverted to "Beijing" in 1949 when the People's Republic of China was founded.

(Based on "Names of Beijing", https://en.wikipedia.org/wiki/Names_of_Beijing)

2. The nine gates of the inner city of Beijing are as follows: Xuanwu Gate, Fucheng Gate, Xizhi Gate, Desheng Gate, Anding Gate, Dongzhi Gate, Chaoyang Gate, Chongwen Gate and Zhengyang Gate.

3. I prefer to live in a house in a Siheyuan because there is a courtyard in a Siheyuan where I can plant vegetables and flowers. In addition it is convenient for me to go outside to have a walk in the yard.

Unit 7
Beijing in History

Section A Reading and Writing

Task 1 **Skimming and Scanning**

(1) N   (2) N   (3) N   (4) Y   (5) N   (6) NG   (7) N

(8) to achieve maximum harmony between the human and natural world.

(9) (China's last imperial line) the Qing Dynasty

(10) live near the eight gates of the Inner City

Task 2 **Thinking and Writing**

Sample Writing

Qianmen

Qianmen, formerly named as Lizhengmen (丽正门), is the colloquial name for Zhengyangmen (正阳门). The gate, once guarding the southern entry into the Inner City, is situated to the south of Tiananmen Square, which remains an important geographical marker of the city.

Qianmen was first built in 1419 during the Ming Dynasty and once consisted of the gatehouse proper and an archery tower, which were connected by side walls and formed a large barbican together with side gates. The gate guarded the direct entry into the imperial city. It sustained considerable damage when the Eight-Power Allied Force invaded the city, and its complex was extensively reconstructed in 1914.

After the Communist victory in 1949, the Qianmen gatehouse was occupied by the Beijing garrison of the People's Liberation Army and vacated in 1980, which has now become a tourist attraction. At 42 metres high, the Qianmen gatehouse remains the tallest of all gates in Beijing's city wall. Qianmen gatehouse survived the demolition of city walls in the late 1960's during the construction of the Beijing Subway.

The Qianmen is situated on the central north-south axis of Beijing. The kilometer zero point of highways in China is located just outside the Qianmen Gate. (208 words)

Task 3 **Research and Development**

One Day Bus Tour: Beijing Hutong, Lama Temple, Panda zoo

1. Itinerary

(1) Pick you up at the south gate of your university at 7:20 am, and then drive to Beijing Zoo to see the lovely Giant Pandas as well as other animals (about 40 minutes).

(2) Take you to the Lama Temple, the largest and most perfectly preserved lamasery of Gelug Sect in present Beijing. Two-hour tour for the mysterious Tibet style Buddhism temple, finished at about 12:00.

(3) Have lunch with locals in a typical Beijing resident's house.

(4) Visit the old Beijing lanes by taking rickshaws. Hutong tour lasts for 2 hours, in

which you can explore the real life of ordinary people in Beijing.

(5) Head to the Olympic Stadium where you have about 45 minutes to take pictures at the Bird's Nest and the Water Cube.

(6) On the way to your university, the short visit to a China Tea House is arranged to enjoy tea ceremony. Transfer back to your university.

2. **Price including** (Tips to the guide and driver are excluded):

(1) Pick-up and drop-off service from your hotel;

(2) Air-conditioned vehicle van with driver;

(3) Entrance tickets of sightseeing;

(4) English speaking tour guide explains the sightseeing about the tour;

(5) A typical Chinese lunch.

Section B Listening and Speaking

Task 1   Listening and Speaking

(1) When was the Forbidden City built?
   It was built between 1406 and 1420 during the Ming Dynasty.

(2) How many emperors lived in the Forbidden City in the history?
   Twenty-four emperors of the Ming and Qing dynasties.

(3) Why was the Forbidden City built?
   It was built as a means of protection for the Chinese emperor and his family.

(4) Is it true that there are 9,999.5 rooms in the Forbidden City?
   No, the 9,999 rooms and a half is just a myth. By the last count, including big and small palaces, halls, towers, pavilions, belvederes, there are 8,707 rooms.

(5) Why are many gates inside the imperial city decorated with gilded doornails counted by 9?
   The reason is that "9" was regarded as the biggest number in ancient China and it was used to imply the emperor, resembling the imperial power in a symbolic sense.

Task 2   Vocabulary Building

(1) originally   (2) associated   (3) administrative   (4) explanation

(5) residential   (6) opposite   (7) exposure   (8) privacy

(9) ritualistic   (10) historic

Unit 7
Beijing in History

参考译文

(1) Beijing, the capital city, is the political, cultural and administrative center of the People's Republic of China, as well as a fascinating metropolis that mixes the old and new. Beijing, as a settlement, has a history of more than 3,000 years. It is one of the few inland capitals(内陆首都) in the world that are not built beside a major river, which owes its long prominence to its strategic geographical position. Beijing majestically reposes on the northmost part of the North China Plain(华北平原); to the northwest lie Shanxi Province and the Inner Mongolian Steppe(内蒙古大草原), and towards the east is the Bohai Sea(渤海).

(2) Hutongs are a type of narrow streets or alleys, commonly associated with northern Chinese cities, most prominently Beijing. In Beijing, many neighborhoods were formed by joining one Chinese quadrangle (siheyuan) to another to form a hutong, and then joining one hutong to another. Hutongs represent an important cultural element of the city of Beijing. Thanks to Beijing's long history and status as the capital for six dynasties, almost every hutong has its anecdotes, and some are even associated with historic events. In contrast to the court life(宫廷生活) and elite culture represented by the Forbidden City(紫禁城), the Summer Palace(颐和园), and the Temple of Heaven(天坛), the hutongs reflect the culture of grassroots Beijingers.

Unit 8

Leisure

> **导 读**
>
> 本单元旨在通过对中国茶文化、传统音乐、围棋和书法的简要介绍，使学生加深对中华休闲文化的理解，掌握相关的语言表达方式，在对外交流过程中更好的宣扬本民族的文化。

Before You Start

While you are preparing for this unit, think about the following questions:
1. Do you like drinking tea? Why or why not?
2. Among the four traditional arts of Qin (a string musical instrument), Qi (a strategic board game), Shu (calligraphy) and Hua (painting), which would you like to practice for fun and relaxation?

Section A Reading and Writing

Text 1   Tea Culture

Chinese people are believed to have enjoyed tea drinking for more than 4000 years. ①Legend has it that Yan Di, one of the three rulers in ancient times, tasted all kinds of herbs to find medical cures. One day, as he was being poisoned by some herb he had ingested, a drop of water from a tea tree dripped into his mouth and he was saved. For a long time, tea was used as a herbal medicine. During the Western Zhou Dynasty, it was a religious offering. During the Spring and Autumn Period, people ate fresh tea leaves as vegetables. With the popularization of Buddhism from the Three Kingdoms to the Northern and Southern Dynasties, its

refreshing effect made it a favorite among monks in Zazen meditation(坐禅).

Tea as a drink prospered during the Tang Dynasty, and tea shops became popular. A major event of this time was the completion of *Tea Classics*(《茶经》), the cornerstone of Chinese tea culture, by Lu Yu(陆羽), Tea Sage of China. ②The book details rules concerning various aspects of tea, such as growth areas for tea trees, wares and skills for processing and tasting of tea, the history of Chinese tea and quotations from other records, comments on tea from various places, and notes on what occasions tea wares should be complete and when some wares could be omitted.

Tinted by the cultural style of the Song Dynasty, tea culture at this time was delicate and sumptuous(奢华的). New skills created many different ways to enjoy tea. The Ming Dynasty laid the foundation for tea processing, types and drinking styles that we have inherited.

During the Qing Dynasty folk art entered tea shops, making them popular entertainment centers. This habit is still practiced in Chengdu, Sichuan Province.

During the Tang Dynasty, a Japanese monk brought tea seeds from Zhejiang Province to Japan. Later in the Southern Song Dynasty, Zen① (禅宗) masters brought tea procedures and wares from China to Japan, promoting the initiation of the Japanese tea ceremony. In the Song Dynasty, Arabic merchants exported tea from Quanzhou, Fujian Province. In the Ming Dynasty, tea was sold to Southeast Asian and South African countries. In 1610 it went to Europe via Macau in a Dutch merchant ship. Thus it became an international drink.

There are four basic steps to select tea.

1. *Observe*. ③Good or fresh tea has a green luster in a tight shape, but poor tea is loose and dull. The leaves should be dry enough to make a rustling(沙沙声) noise in the palm.

2. *Smell*. ④The fragrance should be pure without a charred taste or acid smell. Good tea leaves, especially fresh ones, have a natural aroma like orchid(兰花) or jasmine(茉莉) while the poor ones smell stale.

3. *Taste*. You can taste the leaves by chewing them carefully. Good tea leaves have a fresh mellowness(醇香). You can also infuse(沏、泡) some to see if the leaves unfold smoothly and sink slowly to the bottom. Good tea liquor is emerald(翠绿色的) green or golden. It has a tint of bitterness with a lasting sweet aftertaste. Stale liquor is malodorous (有难闻气味的) and dark brown.

---

① 禅宗,汉传佛教宗派之一,中晚唐之后成为汉传佛教的主流和最主要的象征之一。其核心思想为:"不立文字,教外别传;直指人心,见性成佛"。意指透过自身修证,从日常生活中参究真理,直到最后悟道,也就是真正认识自己的本来面目。禅宗在中国佛教各宗派中流传时间最长,影响甚广,在中国哲学思想及艺术思想上有着重要的影响。

4. *See* the infused tea leaves. The infused leaves should be even without impurity.

After you purchase good tea, keep it in a dry cool place, avoiding direct sunshine. An airtight container is a good choice. Avoid putting teas of different aromas too close. (565 words)

(Based on: http://www.travelchinaguide.com/intro/cuisine_drink/tea/)

Difficult Sentences

① Legend has it that Yan Di, one of the three rulers in ancient times, tasted all kinds of herbs to find medical cures.

相传,古代三皇之一的炎帝尝百草、寻医药。

② The book details rules concerning various aspects of tea, such as growth areas for tea trees, wares and skills for processing and tasting of tea, the history of Chinese tea and quotations from other records, comments on tea from various places, and notes on what occasions tea wares should be complete and when some wares could be omitted.

该书详细论述了与茶有关的方方面面,比如茶树的种植区域、制茶及品茶的器皿和技巧、中国的茶历史及其他史料、各地所产茶之优劣,书中还提到了什么场合应使用整套茶具、什么场合某些茶具可以省略。

③ Good or fresh tea has a green luster in a tight shape, but poor tea is loose and dull.

好茶叶或者新鲜的茶叶带有绿色的光泽、外形紧结,而劣质茶叶则松散、颜色发暗。

④ The fragrance should be pure without a charred taste or acid smell.

香气应纯正,无焦味或酸味。

Text 2 Traditional Music

Traditional Chinese music can be traced back to 7000—8000 years ago based on the discovery of a bone flute made in the Neolithic Age(新石器时代). In the Xia, Shang and Zhou Dynasties, only royal families and dignitary(权贵的) officials enjoyed music, which was made on chimes(编钟) and bells. During the Tang Dynasty, dancing and singing entered the mainstream, spreading from the royal court to the common people. ①With the introduction of foreign religions such as Buddhism and Islam, exotic and religious melodies were absorbed into Chinese music and were enjoyed by the Chinese people at fairs organized by religious temples.

In the Song Dynasty, original operas such as Zaju① and Nanxi② were performed in tearooms, theatres, and showplaces. Writers and artists liked them so much that Ci, a new type of literature resembling lyrics, thrived. During the Yuan Dynasty, Qu, another

---

① 杂剧最早见于唐代,泛指歌舞以外诸如杂技等各色节目;到了宋代,杂剧已发展成为包括有歌舞、音乐、杂技等多种成分的艺术形式。

② 南戏是宋元时代流行在我国南方地区的用南曲演唱的戏曲艺术。民间俗称戏文,或称为南曲戏文,简称南戏文。南戏为其后许多声腔剧种的兴起和发展奠定了基础,堪称中国的百戏之祖。

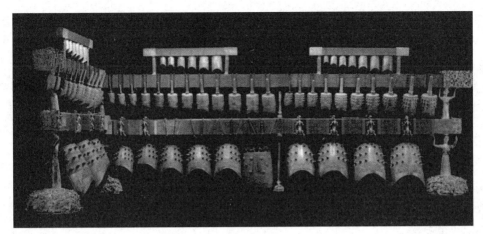

Chimes and Bells

type of literature based on music became popular. This was also a period when many traditional musical instruments were developed such as the Pipa（琵琶）, the Chinese flute (Di) and the Chinese Zither(Zheng)（筝）.

During the Ming and Qing Dynasties, the art of traditional opera developed rapidly and diversely in different regions. ② When these distinctive opera styles were performed at the capital (now called Beijing), artists combined the essence of the different styles and created Beijing Opera, one of the three cornerstones of Chinese culture (the other two being Chinese medicine and traditional Chinese painting) which continue to be appreciated even in modern times.

Besides these types, Chinese peasants were clever enough to compose folk songs, which also developed independently with local flavor. Folk songs described working and daily life such as fishing, farming, and herding and were very popular among the common people.

Traditional Musical Instruments

◆ **Chinese Lute（Pipa）**

Originally named after the loquat（枇杷）fruit, the earliest Pipa known was found to have been made in the Qin Dynasty. By the Tang Dynasty, the Pipa had reached its summit. It was loved by everyone—from the royal court to the common folk—and it occupied a predominant place in the orchestra. Many well-known writers and poets created poems and mentioned it in their works. Bai Juyi, the master poet, vividly depicted the performance like this: rapid and soft notes mingled were just like big and small pearls dropping onto the jade plates①.

Afterwards, the Pipa underwent improvement in playing

---

① 大诗人白居易形象地对琵琶演奏这样描述：嘈嘈切切错杂弹，大珠小珠落玉盘。

techniques and structure. ③Players then changed from holding the Pipa transversely(横着) to holding it vertically(垂直地), and from using a pick to using the fingers to pluck the strings directly. In modern times, the volume and resonance have also been improved. The traditional work "Spring Moonlight on the Flowers by the River"(春江花月夜), which has a history of over one hundred years, has brought harmony and a sense of beauty to untold numbers of people.

◆ **Erhu**

The Erhu, also called "Huqin", was introduced from the western region during the Tang Dynasty. During the Song Dynasty, it was refined and improved and new variations appeared. It was also an important instrument for playing the melody of Beijing Opera.

When playing, the player usually stands the Erhu on his lap, and moves the bow(乐弓) across the vertical strings. The well-known music "Moon Reflection in the Second Spring"(二泉映月) was created by the blind folk artist Hua Yanjun, also named A Bing by the people. Though he could not see anything of the world, he played his Erhu with his heart and imagination. This melody conjures up(唤起对……的想象) a poetic night scene under the moonlight and expresses the composer's desolation and hope.

◆ **Chinese Flute(Di)**

The earliest Chinese flute was made from bone over 7,000 years ago. Since then, most flutes have been made of bamboo and they also come in wood, jade, and iron. By blowing airstreams through a hole while opening and closing other holes with flexibly moving fingers, a player can produce leisurely and mellifluous(甜蜜流畅的) sounds that seem like they are from far away. This always reminds people of a pastoral picture of a farmer riding on a bull while playing a flute. (678 words)

(Based on: http://www.travelchinaguide.com/intro/arts/chinese-music.htm)

Difficult Sentences

① With the introduction of foreign religions such as Buddhism and Islam, exotic and religious melodies were absorbed into Chinese music and were enjoyed by the Chinese people at fairs organized by religious temples.
随着佛教、伊斯兰教等外国宗教传入中国,异域的宗教旋律被中国音乐所吸收,在庙会上受到了人们的喜爱。

② When these distinctive opera styles were performed at the capital (now called Beijing),

artists combined the essence of the different styles and created Beijing opera, one of the three cornerstones of Chinese culture (the other two being Chinese medicine and traditional Chinese painting) which continue to be appreciated even in modern times.
当这些别具特色的戏剧种类在都城(今北京)演出时,艺术家把各剧种的精华融合在一起创造了中国文化三大基石之一的京剧(另外两个是中药和国画),至今仍然受到人们的喜爱。

③ Players then changed from holding the Pipa transversely to holding it vertically, and from using a pick to using the fingers to pluck the strings directly. In modern times, the volume and resonance have also been improved.
之后演奏者将琵琶由横握变成竖弹,弃拨片而直接用手指拨弦。音量和共鸣在现代也得到了改进。

Exercises

Task 1 Thinking and Judging

Directions: *Read Text 1 and judge whether the following statements are true (T) or false (F).*

(　) (1) Tea was discovered by Yan Di.
(　) (2) Tea had been put to various uses before it was widely consumed as a drink.
(　) (3) Tea processing skills are not dealt with in *Tea Classics*.
(　) (4) The Ming Dynasty witnessed tea shops' prosperity as an entertainment center.
(　) (5) Good tea smells fresh and fragrant, tastes sweet after a tint of bitterness.

Task 2 Vocabulary Building

Directions: *Complete the following paragraph with the words listed below. Change the forms if necessary.*

| solemn | depict | horn | version | breakout |
| grand | classical | flip | title | accompany |

"Ambush from All Sides"(十面埋伏) is a ___(1)___ piece of lute music about the decisive battle in 202 B.C. between the two armies of Chu and Han. The currently popular ___(2)___ consists of a number of short sections, each with a generalized ___(3)___. The beginning sections of the music focus on the description of the mighty and ___(4)___ battle array of the Han Army. The music in these sections is high-spirited and powerful, ___(5)___ by the sounds of drums and ___(6)___. The beat of drums quickened gradually to create a tense explosive atmosphere before the ___(7)___ of the full-scale battles. Then comes the main body of the music, which is changeable and rapid. The techniques of ___(8)___, sweeping, circular fingering, wringing, rolling, and halting are employed to represent the furious battle between the armies of Chu and Han. The later sections of the music ___(9)___ Xiang Yu's suicide at the Wujiang River after his defeat. The melodies are mournful, ___(10)___ and stirring, bringing out a strong artistic image of Xiang Yu. The desolation and sadness contrast sharply with the triumphant climax for the victor. Today "Ambush from All Sides" still remains one of the most popular lute music pieces in all kinds of concerts in China.

Task 3 Discussing and Writing

Directions: *Write a short essay on Tea Classification.*

Section B Listening and Speaking

Text 3 Situational Dialogue: About Go(围棋)

Host: Go is a strategic board game that has been popular in East Asia for nearly 3,000 years. It is known as Weiqi in Chinese, Igo in Japanese and Baduk in Korean. Here with me today is Daniel, an amateur go player. He is going to tell us more about this ancient game.

Daniel: Besides being one of the oldest board games known to man, go is also considered as one of the most logical and intelligent.

H: Are there complex rules?

D: Actually the rules are very simple and they remained essentially unchanged throughout history. The game starts with an empty board.

H: That's funny. In chess, we start with everything we have on the board. What does the go board look like?

D: The standard one is marked with a grid of 19 lines by 19 lines. Smaller 9×9 and 13×13 boards are for beginners.

H: How about the pieces?

D: They're called stones. One player has a supply of black stones, the other a supply of white. The players take turns, placing one stone at each turn on a vacant point. Black plays first.

H: Where to put the stones? In the squares?

D: No, on the intersections(交叉点) of the lines. Once played, stones are not moved.

But they may be surrounded and so captured, in which case they are removed from the board as prisoners.

H: What do players want to achieve in a game?

D: Go is a territorial game. The main objective is to win as much territory as possible.

H: How to decide who controls a larger area?

D: ①At the end of the game the players count one point for each vacant intersection inside their own territory, and one point for every stone they have captured. The one with the larger total is the winner.

H: Seems not hard to understand.

D: But once these basic rules are grasped, go shows its staggering depth. The strategic and tactical possibilities of the game are endless. ②It reflects the skills of the players in balancing attack and defense, making stones work efficiently, remaining flexible in response to changing situations, timing, analyzing accurately and recognizing the strengths and weaknesses of the opponent.

H: No wonder some say go is not merely a casual pastime for the idle hour, it is also an exercise in abstract reasoning, a mental workout and a mirror of one's personality.

D: Yeah, for me it's a way of life. (408 words)

Difficult Sentences

① At the end of the game the players count one point for each vacant intersection inside their own territory, and one point for every stone they have captured.
棋局结束时,双方各自地盘内一方棋子所围的每一空白交叉点算一目,所提对方的子,一个子算一目。
〔注:围棋的胜负判定是靠目数(通常一个交叉点算一目)来比的,即谁围的交叉点多,谁就获胜。围棋中把无气之子提出盘外的手段叫"提子"。〕

② It reflects the skills of the players in balancing attack and defense, making stones work efficiently, remaining flexible in response to changing situations, timing, analyzing accurately and recognizing the strengths and weaknesses of the opponent.
它反映出棋手在攻守平衡、行棋效率、随机应变、时机把握、准确分析以及识别对手优缺点等方面的能力。

Text 4 An Introduction to Chinese Calligraphy

Chinese calligraphy (Brush calligraphy) is an art unique to Asian cultures. Qin (a string musical instrument), Qi (a strategic board game), Shu (calligraphy), and Hua (painting) are the four basic skills and disciplines of the Chinese literati(文人学士).

Regarded as the most abstract and elegant form of art in Chinese culture, calligraphy is often thought to be most revealing of one's personality. ①During the imperial era, calligraphy was used as an important criterion for selection of executives to the imperial court. Unlike other visual art techniques, all calligraphy strokes are permanent and incorrigible(不可修正的), demanding careful planning and confident execution. Such are the skills required for an administrator/executive. While one has to conform to the defined structure of words, the expression can be extremely creative. ②To exercise humanistic imagination and touch under the merciless laws and regulations is also a virtue well appreciated.

③By controlling the concentration of ink, the thickness and absorptivity(吸收性) of the paper, and the flexibility of the brush, the artist is free to produce an infinite variety of styles and forms. In contrast to western calligraphy, diffusing ink blots and dry brush strokes are viewed as a natural impromptu expression rather than a fault. ④While western calligraphy often pursue font-like uniformity, homogeneity of characters in one size is only a craft. To the artist, calligraphy is a mental exercise that coordinates the mind and the body to choose the best styling in expressing the content of the passage. It is a most relaxing yet highly disciplined exercise indeed for one's physical and spiritual well being. Historically, many calligraphy artists were well-known for their longevity.

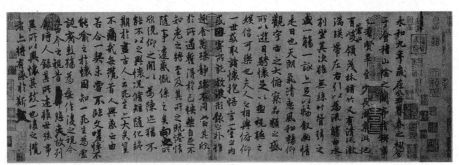

唐代 冯承素摹的《兰亭序》纸本,称《神龙本兰亭》,现北京故宫博物院收藏,高24.5厘米,宽69.9厘米,公认为是最好的摹本,被视为珍品。

Brush calligraphy is not only loved and practiced by Chinese. Koreans and Japanese equally adore calligraphy as an important treasure of their heritage. Many Japanese schools still have the tradition of having a student contest of writing characters at the beginning of a new school year. A biannual(一年二次的) gathering commemorating the "Lan Ting Ji Xu"① by Wang Xizhi (the most famous Chinese calligrapher in the Jin Dynasty) is said to be held ceremonially in Japan. There is a national award of Wang Xizhi prize for the best calligraphy artist. Not too long ago, Korean government officials were required to excel in

---

① 王羲之的《兰亭集序》。当时有26人赋诗41首,并聚诗成集。王羲之于酒酣之际乘兴用鼠须笔在蚕茧纸上为诗集写了这篇序,记下了诗宴盛况和观感。全文28行,324字,通篇遒媚飘逸,字字精妙,有如神助。像其中的20个"之"字,竟无一雷同,成为书法史上的一绝,有"天下第一行书"之称,是中国晋代书法成就的代表。

calligraphy. The office of Okinawa(冲绳) governor still displays a large screen of Chinese calligraphy as a dominating decor.

In the West, Picasso① and Matisse② are two artists who openly declared the influence by Chinese calligraphy on their works. Picasso once said that if he were born a Chinese, he would have been a calligraphy artist rather than a painter. (429 words)

(Based on http://www.asiawind.com/art/callig/Default.htm)

Difficult Sentences

① During the imperial era, calligraphy was used as an important criterion for selection of executives to the imperial court.
在帝王时代,书法是封建王朝选拔官员的一个重要标准。

② To exercise humanistic imagination and touch under the merciless laws and regulations is also a virtue well appreciated.
在铁面无私的律法面前表现出人文想象和人文情怀同样是种备受推崇的美德。

③ By controlling the concentration of ink, the thickness and absorptivity of the paper, and the flexibility of the brush, the artist is free to produce an infinite variety of styles and forms.
通过墨的浓淡、纸张的厚度和吸水性,还有毛笔的柔软,艺术家能随心所欲地创造出变化无穷的风格和形态。

④ While western calligraphy often pursue font-like uniformity, homogeneity of characters in one size is only a craft.
西方书法往往追求字体上的一致,而汉字保持大小均衡则不过是一种技艺罢了。

Exercises

Task 1 Listening and Summarizing

Directions: *Listen to Text 3 and fill in the blanks with what you hear from the recording. Use NO MORE THAN THREE words for each blank.*

Go is one of the world's great __(1)__ games and originated over 3,000 years ago in China. By all appearances, it's just two players taking turns __(2)__ on a 19×19 (or smaller) grid of intersections. Go is a __(3)__ game, he who controls a larger area is the winner. The rules are very __(4)__ but there's plenty of choice to move the stones, with countless __(5)__ possibilities. This is where the charm of the game lies. It is a game that combines science, art and competition.

---

① 毕加索·帕布罗(1881—1973)西班牙画家,20世纪最多产和最有影响的画家之一。
② 亨利·马蒂斯(1869—1954)法国著名画家,野兽派的创始人和主要代表人物,也是一位雕塑家、版画家。他以使用鲜明、大胆的色彩而著名。

Task 2 Listening and Understanding

Directions: *Listen to Text 4 and number the topics in the order you hear them.*

a. Calligraphy improves mental and physical health.

b. Careful planning and confident execution are needed in calligraphy.

c. Diffusing ink blots and dry brush strokes are not seen as a fault in Chinese calligraphy.

d. Calligraphic works reflect a person's personality.

e. Brush calligraphy is loved by people from diverse cultures.

f. Chinese calligraphy is a very creative form of visual arts.

Task 3 Dialogue Making

Directions: *You are telling a foreign friend how to practice brush calligraphy. Make up a dialogue and then act it out with your partners.*

Translation Practice

Directions: *Translate the following passages into English.*

(1) 茶之为物,能引导我们进入一个默想人生的世界。采茶必须天气清明的清早,当山上的空气极为清新,露水的芬芳尚留于叶上时,所采的茶叶方称上品。因此,茶是凡间纯洁的象征,在采制烹煮(infusion)的手续中,都须十分清洁。采摘烘焙(fermenting),烹煮取饮之时,手上或杯壶中略有油腻不洁,便会使它丧失美味。所以也只有在眼前和心中毫无富丽繁华的景象和念头时,方能真正的享受它。(节选自林语堂《茶与交友》)

(2) 书法作品跟舞蹈艺术一样可以展现肢体和动作的美感。相互之间能吸收灵感。张旭,唐代草书(cursive-script calligraphy)大家,以韵律独特和风格豪放而著称。传说,他观舞蹈名家公孙一舞而悟,书法大有长进。舞者通过独特的节奏和利落的动作展示了诸如活泼、喜悦、悲伤、愤怒、渴望、需求、勇气和灵感等多种魅力和和情感。张旭草书、李白诗歌和裴旻剑舞被当朝皇帝誉为三绝。

Words and Expressions for Life of Leisure
中华休闲文化相关词汇与表达方式

Za-Zen meditation	坐禅
Tea Classics	《茶经》
Tea Sage of China	中国茶圣
processing and tasting of tea	茶的加工和品茗
tea wares	茶具
tea ceremony	茶道

a charred taste or acid smell	焦味或酸味
a tint of bitterness	微苦
a lasting sweet aftertaste	持久的回甜
green tea	绿茶
black tea	红茶
oolong tea	乌龙茶
Pu-erh tea	普洱茶
scented tea	花茶
chime	编钟
zither	筝
lute (Pipa)	琵琶
resonance	共鸣
bow	乐弓
string	琴弦
board game	棋牌游戏
stone	围棋棋子
capture a stone	提掉一子
diffusing ink blots	晕开的墨渍
dot	点
horizontal stroke, dash	横
vertical stroke, perpendicular downstroke	竖
left-downward stroke, downstroke to the left	撇
right-downward stroke, wavelike stroke	捺
turning stroke, bend, twist	折
hook stroke	钩
right-upward stroke, upstroke to the right	提

Key to Unit 8 Exercises

Before You Start

1. Sample: I drink a lot of tea. I love the aromas of various flavors of tea; holding onto a hot tea mug warms my hands on a cold winter morning; chatting with friends over tea is a great way to relax.

2. Sample: I personally believe that if there's one thing you should learn in your

lifetime, it's how to play an instrument. It not only improves hand-eye coordination but helps the mind to be alert and remain active, which eventually helps to sharpen the memory. Another reason is that music can relieve stress. Sure, learning to play a musical instrument can be a lot of hard work but there is no denying that it is fun and exciting. The sound combined with the release of creativity and emotion can significantly lower a musician's stress level and promote health.

Section A Reading and Writing

Task 1 Thinking and Judging

(1) F   (2) T   (3) F   (4) F   (5) T

Task 2 Vocabulary Building

(1) classical   (2) version   (3) title   (4) grand   (5) accompanied
(6) horns   (7) breakout   (8) flipping   (9) depict   (10) solemn

Task 3 Discussing and Writing

There are many types of tea in the world. They are mainly classified as green tea, black tea and oolong tea. Other tea types include white tea, yellow tea, Pu-erh tea and scented tea.

(1) Green tea is the variety which keeps the original colour of the tea leaves without fermentation during processing.

(2) Black tea, known as "red tea" in China, is tea fermented before baking; it is a later variety developed on the basis of the green tea.

(3) Oolong tea represents a variety half way between the green and the black teas, being made after partial fermentation. It is a specialty from the provinces on China's southeast coast: Fujian, Guangdong and Taiwan.

Section B Listening and Speaking

Task 1 Listening and Summarizing

(1) strategic board   (2) placing stones
(3) territorial   (4) simple
(5) strategic and tactical

Task 2 Listening and Understanding

(1) d   (2) b   (3) f   (4) c   (5) a   (6) e

Task 3 Dialogue Making

A: It's so great you could come over here. I really have no idea how to use these.
B: Wow, brush, paper, ink. What's the plan?
A: I want to practice Chinese calligraphy. But no idea how to get started.
B: That's easy. Sit down. Do you know how to hold chopsticks?

A: Of course, I love Chinese food.

B: It's quite similar. But the brush should be held vertically. At first, pinch the shaft of the writing brush at the midpoint with your forefinger, middle finger, and thumb, and then lean the back of the ring finger on it.

A: How can I possibly write in such a way?

B: All the five fingers should be crooked. Relax. Yeah, that's it. You may rest your wrist or elbow on the desk to steady your hand for writing. Put it down and try again.

A: What shall I practice writing first?

B: Most beginners start by imitating exemplary models of regular script(楷体).

A: That's a great idea!

参考译文

(1) There is something in the nature of tea that leads us into a world of quiet contemplation(沉思) of life. Picked at early dawn on a clear day, when the morning air on mountain top was clear and thin, and the fragrance of dews was still upon the leaves, tea is still associated with the fragrance and refinement of the magic dew in its enjoyment. Tea is then symbolic(象征的) of earthly purity, requiring the most fastidious(严苛的) cleanliness in its preparation, from picking, fermenting(发酵) and preserving to its final infusion(过滤) and drinking, easily upset or spoiled by the slightest contamination(污染) of oily hands or oily cups. Consequently, its enjoyment is appropriate in an atmosphere where all ostentation (虚饰) or suggestion of luxury is banished(驱逐) from one's eyes and one's thoughts. (Excerpted from "Tea and Friendship" by Lin Yutang)

(2) Calligraphic works can demonstrate the beauty of both the body and movement, like the art of dance. They can absorb inspiration(灵感) from each other. Zhang Xu, a cursive-script calligraphy master of the Tang Dynasty, was famous for distinctive rhythms (韵律) and a wild style. Legend says that he made swift progress in his calligraphy after he got inspiration from a dance performed by the famous dancer Gongsun. Through distinctive rhythms and neat movements, the dancer demonstrated various kinds of charms and emotions such as vividness, joy, sadness, anger, aspiration(愿望), demand, boldness(勇猛) and inspiration. The cursive-script calligraphic works by Zhang Xu, the poems by Li Bai and the sword dance by Pei Min were praised as the three wonders by the emperor of their time.

Unit 9

Virtues

导 读

在中华民族源远流长、博大精深的伦理文化遗产中，许多优良传统美德时至今日依然有着强大的生命力。本单元着重介绍中国传统美德的核心思想以及与生活息息相关的各种优良品格，使学生能够运用所学中国文化知识及相关的英语表达方式进行跨文化交流，弘扬中华民族优良传统与文化。

Before You Start

While you are preparing for this unit, think about the following questions:
1. What do you know about traditional virtues in Chinese culture? Can you list some?
2. What characteristics did traditional Chinese women have? Can you name some famous women of virtue in ancient China?

Section A Reading and Writing

Text 1   The Five Constant Virtues

Owning over thousands of years of history, the Chinese have created a brilliant history and culture, and at the same time have formed their own moral code that has played an important role in social development and progress. This is what we call Traditional Virtues, which still have great significance today and whose value to the development of human civilization is now widely recognized.

Benevolence(仁), righteousness(义), propriety (礼), wisdom (智) and fidelity (信) are the Five Constant Virtues[①](五常) which are the most important ones in traditional China.

---

① 五常中的常是不变的意思，指一定准则。五常就是五条准则，即仁、义、礼、智、信，是用以调整、规范君臣、父子、兄弟、夫妇、朋友等人伦关系的行为准则。与"三纲"(君为臣纲、父为子纲、夫为妻纲)合称"三纲五常"，是中国儒家伦理文化中的架构。

Unit 9
Virtues

They all came from Confucianism (儒家思想) and are widely acknowledged all over China. To be a moral person, the ancient Chinese cultivated and monitored themselves according to the Five Constant Virtues and carried them down to the modern life.

Benevolence (Ren)

Benevolence is the first and most important virtue among the Five Constant Virtues. ①It manifests itself in the inner mind, in love and compassion for people, and in avoiding harm or envy toward anyone. In terms of behavior, benevolence demands that one be amiable, not argue angrily with others nor do evil deeds. To cultivate one's virtue of Benevolence one should use another Confucian version of the Golden Rule: ②What one does not wish for oneself, one ought not to do to anyone else; what one recognizes as desirable for oneself, one ought to be willing to grant to others. ③Virtue, in this Confucian view, is based upon harmony with other people, produced through this type of ethical practice by a growing identification of the interests of self and other. In short, as parents treat their children, the benevolent person spares no effort to help others; one even lays down one's life to this end, with no thought of being repaid.

Righteousness (Yi)

Among his teachings, Confucius emphasized righteousness which is the ability to distinguish between right and wrong. Righteousness can be thought of as similar to what is often referred to as a "conscience" or "justice". Confucius believed that actions should be taken on the basis of whether the act is morally right or wrong as opposed to whether it will provide profit or utility (实用价值) to an individual or group. Above all righteousness is about preserving one's integrity.

Propriety (Li)

Propriety means ceremony or correct behavior. The contents of propriety include loyalty, filial piety (孝顺), fraternal duty, respect, etc. ④Originating in ancient sacrificial rites, propriety, in a general sense, signifies behavioral norms which maintain hierarchy. In ancient society, besides the relation of monarch and subjects (君与臣), there were also the relations of father and sons, husband and wife, the elder and the young, teacher and students, and others. These relations differ but all demand modest respect to others.

Wisdom (Zhi)

Wisdom is the knowledge by which one judges right and wrong, good and evil. The saint defined the personality of "the wise" as "a wise man free from confusions"("智者不惑"). The real man of wisdom shall not only be able to distinguish truth from falsehood, but also be rational and sensible; he shall never get confused in front of profits or different paths. That is to say, the wisdom concerns not only one person's ability and aptitude, but also his moral cultivation. Confucius also pointed out that the acquisition of "wisdom" lies in learning, which can be obtained from both books and life.

Fidelity (Xin)

Fidelity is honesty. This means that, externally, one's deeds match one's words; and that internally one's words and mind are in unison. Fidelity is a key to the perfection of human nature. It is the basis without which other virtues lose their authenticity(真实性); hence they are inseparable. Fidelity is natural in a child, but might be lost due to external influences. (610 words)

(Based on http://www.foreignercn.com/index.php? option = com _ content&view = article&id = 5,047: the-five-constant-virtues-of-china&catid = 1: history-and-culture&Itemid = 114)

Difficult Sentences

① It manifests itself in the inner mind, in love and compassion for people, and in avoiding harm or envy toward anyone.
仁体现在内心对他人的爱与同情,以及避免伤害和嫉妒他人。

② What one does not wish for oneself, one ought not to do to anyone else; what one recognizes as desirable for oneself, one ought to be willing to grant to others.
已所不欲,勿施于人;已所欲者,亦施于人。

③ Virtue, in this Confucian view, is based upon harmony with other people, produced through this type of ethical practice by a growing identification of the interests of self and other.
儒家学说"仁"的基础是人与人之间的和谐,和谐的人际关系通过践行"仁义"之道,利益求同存异而实现。

④ Originating in ancient sacrificial rites, propriety, in a general sense, signifies behavioral norms which maintain hierarchy.
礼起源于古代祭祀仪式,就一般意义而言象征着包含社会等级的行为规范。

Text 2 Women of Ancient China

Chinese society in Confucian terms was a patriarchal(父系的) society with strict rules of conduct. The women in ancient Chinese culture needed to behave according to the rules set by Confucianism. The traditional ideal woman was a dependant being whose behavior was governed by the "three obediences and four virtues"①(三从四德). The three aspects of obedience were: to obey their father before marriage, their husband during married life, and their son in widowhood. The four virtues were: morality, proper speech, modest manner and diligent work. For thousands of years, people hold the stereotype of Chinese

---

① 三从指未嫁从父、既嫁从夫、夫死从子;四德是妇德、妇言、妇容、妇功。

women as reserved, shy, obedient and subordinate to men. It is well known that women had inferior positions in traditional China. Nevertheless, not all women in Chinese feudal society kept silent in their unfair lives. Some women realized their situations and fought for their rights. ① They created new virtues and images for traditional Chinese women as intelligent, brave, soft, demure and attractive.

Here are a few famous women in the history of China.

The only female emperor——Wu Zetian

Even though according to the Confucian beliefs having a woman rule would be unnatural, during the most glorious years of the Tang dynasty a woman did rule, and ruled successfully. She was Wu Zetian (624—705 AD), the only female in Chinese history to rule as emperor. To some she was an autocrat (独裁者), ruthless in her desire to gain and keep power. To others she, as a woman doing a "man's job," merely did what she had to do, and acted no differently than most male emperors of her day. It's noted that she managed to effectively rule China during one of its most peaceful and culturally diverse periods.

As the only female emperor in the Chinese feudal dynasties, with exceptional wisdom and great talent, Wu Zetian elevated the position of women. She had scholars write biographies of famous women and moved her court away from the seat of traditional male power and tried to establish a new dynasty.

A model mother—Mencius①(孟子)'s mother

Mencius's mother, Zhang-shih (仉氏), is often held up as an exemplary female figure in Chinese culture. ②One of the most famous traditional Chinese four-character idioms is "Three Moves by Mencius's Mother", referring to the story of Zhang-shih moving three times from a house near a graveyard to a market to a butchery, finally to a school before finding a location that she felt was suitable for her child's upbringing. The story tells of the importance of a proper environment for the upbringing of children. It's well believed that Zhang-shih was a woman of very superior virtues, and that her son's subsequent achievement was to a great degree owing to her influence and training.

Three Moves by Mencius's Mother

---

① 孟子(公元前372—前289),名轲,字子舆,战国时期邹国人,中国古代著名思想家、教育家,战国时期儒家代表人物。

A cultural envoy — Princess Wencheng

In 641, when the Tang Dynasty (618—907) was in its time of peace and prosperity, Princess Wencheng of the Tang made her journey to the Tubo Kingdom (吐蕃) as the bride of Songtsan Gampo (松赞干布), the King of Tubo. ③As the peace and culture envoy from Tang, Princess Wencheng paved the way for the spread of Buddhism into Tubo Kingdom by having the Ramoche Monastery built. Meanwhile she also taught Tibetans how to grow crops and vegetables. She brought into the Tubo Kingdom carriages, horses, donkeys and camels, as well as medical works and various kinds of farming and industrial techniques. Under her direction, the Tubo Kingdom experienced fast social progress. ④After Princess Wencheng married into the Tubo Kingdom, the Central Plains (中原) and the Tubo area maintained close relations for more than 200 years, a period almost free from wars and most notable for its varied cultural and commercial exchanges. (604 words)

(Based on http://www.womeninworldhistory.com/heroine6.html
http://history.cultural-china.com/en/48History5,414.html
http://www.china.com.cn/ch-xizang/tibet/picture_album/english/songwen/songwen.html)

Difficult Sentences

① They created new virtues and images for traditional Chinese women as intelligent, brave, soft, demure and attractive.

她们为传统中国女性创造了新的美德与形象：聪明勇敢、温婉端庄、富于魅力。

② One of the most famous traditional Chinese four-character idioms is 'Three Moves by Mencius's Mother', referring to the story of Zhang-shih moving three times from a house near a graveyard to a market to a butchery, finally to a school before finding a location that she felt was suitable for her child's upbringing.

中国最著名的四字成语之一"孟母三迁"讲述了仉（音 zhǎng）氏为了给孩子寻找良好的教育环境前后三次迁居，分别从墓地附近迁至市场再至屠宰场附近，最终迁至她认为适于孩子成长的私塾附近。

③ As the peace and culture envoy from Tang, Princess Wencheng paved the way for the spread of Buddhism into Tubo Kingdom by having the Ramoche Monastery built.

作为大唐的和平与文化使者，文成公主修建了小昭寺，为佛教在吐蕃王国的传播铺平了道路。

④ After Princess Wencheng married into the Tubo Kingdom, the Central Plains and the Tubo area maintained close relations for more than 200 years, a period almost free from wars and most notable for its varied cultural and commercial exchanges.

文成公主嫁入吐蕃之后，中原与吐蕃地区维持了二百余年的友好关系，这一时期几乎没有战乱，以各种文化和商贸交流著称。

Unit 9
Virtues

Exercises

Task1 Skimming and Scanning

Directions: *In this part, you will have 10 minutes to go over Text 1 quickly, then answer the following questions.*

For questions 1—7, mark

Y (for YES) if the statement agrees with the information given in the passage;

N (for NO) if the statement contradicts the information given in the passage;

NG (for NOT GIVEN) if the information is not given in the passage.

For questions 8—10, complete the sentences with the information given in the passage.

(   ) (1) The morality of Chinese in modern society has been significantly influenced by the traditional virtues.

(   ) (2) Confucius was thought to be the first person to create the Five Constant Virtues which were the essence of Confucianism.

(   ) (3) A person with benevolence will not hurt or envy other people and instead he will show love and sympathy to them.

(   ) (4) Benevolence means a person needs to demand others' benefits matched with his own.

(   ) (5) To judge a person's righteousness is to consider whether his act will bring any profit to himself or a group.

(   ) (6) Propriety is based on hierarchy in the society and the family, including different behavioral norms.

(   ) (7) Whatever relations a person is in, he needs to show respect to others according to the rule of propriety.

(8) A person with wisdom should not only be rational and sensible, but also have the ability to tell _____.

(9) Wisdom is a person's moral cultivation, which can be learned from _____.

(10) Fidelity is the unison of one's _____, without which other virtues cannot be carried on.

Task 2 Discussing and Writing

Directions: *Traditional Chinese virtues are fading out among young people. Some people say that it is not necessary to hold traditional virtues, because many of them are out of date as the society develops and changes fast. Do you agree with them or not? You should write a composition of about 200 words to state your point of view.*

Task 3 Reading and Blank-Filling

Directions: *Read the passage of Text 2 and then fill in the blanks.*

(1) In ancient China, women needed to behave appropriately by _____ set by Confucianism.

(2) Four virtues of traditional Chinese women refer to _____.

(3) Although people thought traditional Chinese women should be reserved and obedient to men, some well-known women in the history had _____ for them.

(4) Wu Zetian might have shown her desire to get and keep power, but she just acted _____ most male emperors of her day to rule China.

(5) Wu Zetian had raised the social status of women by _____.

(6) In order to find a proper environment to foster her child, Mencius's mother _____.

(7) Mencius's achievement was to a large extent attributed to _____.

(8) A major significance of Princess Wencheng marrying Songtsan Gampo was that she functioned as _____ for Tang.

(9) Princess Wencheng not only brought resources for agriculture but also facilitated to _____ in Tubo Kingdom by having the Romoche Monastery built.

(10) Princess Wencheng contributed greatly to the close relations between the Central Plains and the Tubo for over 200 years, a period famous for its _____.

Task 4 Translating

Directions: *Translate the following expressions or phrases about women into English.*

(1) 女子无才便是德
(2) 女为悦己者容
(3) 嫁鸡随鸡嫁狗随狗
(4) 三个女人一台戏
(5) 贤妻良母

Section B Listening and Speaking

Text 3 Situational Dialogue: About Filial Piety in China

(*J: Jennet, an American student learning Chinese in China; L: Li Yang, a Chinese student*)

J: Hi, Li Yang. How was your holiday?

L: It's good. I had a great time with my family at my hometown. My grandfather just had his 80th birthday.

J: He must have been very happy to see you back. Does he live with your parents?

L: Yes. Actually not only my grandparents and

parents but also my uncles along with their families all live together.

J: That's incredible! This kind of extended family is very rare nowadays.

L: Yes. But in my hometown we still keep the tradition that several generations share the same dwelling. I grew up with my extended family members and we are still very close to each other. And since I was a little kid, my parents taught me to show filial piety to the seniors in the family.

J: Filial piety? Is that the respect shown to parents?

L: Yes. But it's beyond the respect.

J: Tell me about it. That must be very interesting.

L: Well, filial piety, or *xiao* in Chinese, is a concept originating from Confucianism. It outlines the way in which family members should interact with each other and it's based on a hierarchical relationship.

J: What does it mean?

L: In the family, the elders have the responsibility to care for the young and raise them properly; while the young in turn have the responsibility to respect and obey the elders. For example, my grandparents were great people. ①They were illiterate but they strained every nerve to afford their three children's schooling. And my grandpa has the absolute authority at home.

J: Your grandparents were awesome and foresighted.

L: Yes. Now they are aging, so my parents and uncles are taking care of them by turns.

J: But it needs great patience and compassion to look after the elders, especially when they are at such an age.

L: That's true. But it is a traditional Chinese virtue for younger family members to care for their parents when they get old and no longer work. And in modern society, filial piety breaks down into several key responsibilities. Parents and elders have the responsibility to provide for children and raise them to have the appropriate qualities. This includes teaching them how to be a good person, giving them every opportunity they possibly can, such as enrolling them in good schools, smoothing the way for them to get a job and so on.

J: How about young people?

L: In return for the care and material goods, children and younger family members are expected to be obedient and to make the most of the opportunities elders give them. By doing this and becoming successful, they can bring pride or "face" to the family.

J: No wonder I find Chinese students really work very hard. I guess they don't want to let their parents down.

L: Well, it's true. ②And what's more, to follow filial piety younger family members are also expected to produce children to continue the family line. So you can easily find Chinese parents would urge their children to get married and have babies, especially when their children are over 30.

J: Aha, that's quite interesting. But it's understandable.

L: Yeah. After all, parents always hope their children would have a happy and stable life.

J: I find filial piety has been reflected in various aspects of Chinese life and represents your family and social values. It should be preserved and passed onto generations.

L: It will. We think people are born into a family or a group and cannot prosper alone; the success of an individual depends on the harmony and strength of the group. Family is the core group of the whole society.

J: I agree with you. It's so nice talking with you. I wish I had the chance to visit your large family in future.

L: Ha, you are warmly welcome! (646 words)

Difficult Sentences

① They were illiterate but they strained every nerve to afford their three children's schooling.

他们都不识字,但是却竭尽全力让三个孩子接受教育。

② And what's more, to follow filial piety younger family members are also expected to produce children to continue the family line.

而且,为了尽孝道,家里的年轻一辈都要按照老人的愿望生儿育女,以传承香火。

Text 4　An Introduction to Four Gentlemen in Plants

In ancient China, people called a man of great virtue a gentleman. In the world of flowers, plums（梅）, orchids（兰）, bamboos and chrysanthemums（菊）are known as the four gentlemen in China because these plants' natural characters have something in common with human virtues. ①They have all long been featured in ancient paintings and poems used to express loftiness, righteousness, modesty and purity by Chinese literati（文人）.

Unit 9
Virtues

Pictures of Four Gentlemen in Plants（四君子）

Plum

The plum tree is renowned for bursting into blossoms in the dead of winter. Its subtle fragrance spills forth at one of the coldest times of the year, making it difficult to go unnoticed. Though neither the plum tree nor its blossoms are very striking, they manage to show beautiful elegance during the desolation of winter. ②The character of the plum tree thereby often serves as a metaphor for inner beauty and strength under adverse conditions.

Orchid

Grown in deep mountain valleys, the orchid is one of the top ten well-known flowers in China. ③With delicate fragrance refreshing people's minds, and the elegant figures swaying slightly in the wind, orchids are equal to elegance in Chinese people's eyes. The greatest orchid painter was Zheng Banqiao（郑板桥）in the Qing Dynasty（清朝 1636—1912）who attached great importance to the nature of orchids. He had a preference for painting wild orchids.

Bamboo

In traditional Chinese culture, the bamboo is a metaphor of vitality（生命力）and longevity, which usually relates to a man who has exemplary conduct and nobility of character. The stalk of the bamboo is hollow, which comes to symbolize tolerance and open-mindedness. ④Furthermore, the flexibility and strength of the bamboo stalk also comes to represent the human values of cultivation and integrity in which one yields but does not break.

Their firm and unyielding willpower was admired by many ancient literati and painters. The famous poet Su Shi① once wrote down "Rather eat without meat than live

---

① 苏轼(1037—1101),北宋文学家、书画家。字子瞻,号东坡居士。

without bamboo①(宁可食无肉,不可居无竹)" in his poem to express his deep love for bamboo.

Chrysanthemum

The chrysanthemum is a traditional flower loved by Chinese people, which was planted as early as three thousand years ago. ⑤When nearly all the flowers are withered and bare in late autumn, only chrysanthemums withstand the heavy frost and bloom energetically in graceful shapes and bright colors.

Chrysanthemums have been given more meanings under the pen of literati. The most well-known poem about chrysanthemums is "Plucking chrysanthemums under the eastern hedge, I calmly view the southern hills ②(采菊东篱下,悠然见南山)", which comes from the famous poet Tao Yuanming's poem "Drinking", showing the leisure of Tao's reclusive (隐居的) life.

Known as the four gentlemen, plums, orchids, bamboos and chrysanthemums have become a cultural symbol to label one's moral integrity, not only because of their elegant nature but also thanks to the appreciation and high praise from the painters and literati of different dynasties. (454 words)

(Based on http://culture.chinese.cn/en/article/2009-11/03/content_43290.htm
http://www.chinaonlinemuseum.com/painting-four-gentlemen.php)

Difficult Sentences

① They have all long been featured in ancient paintings and poems used to express loftiness, righteousness, modesty and purity by Chinese literati
一直以来,它们都是中国文人在古代绘画和诗歌中重点描绘的对象,用来表达崇高、正直、谦虚和纯洁。

② The character of the plum tree thereby often serves as a metaphor for inner beauty and strength under adverse conditions.
因此梅花的特点常用来比喻在逆境中体现出的内在美与力量。

③ With delicate fragrance refreshing people's minds, and the elegant figures swaying slightly in the wind, orchids are equal to elegance in Chinese people's eyes.
兰花因其沁人心脾的迷人芬芳和风中轻轻摇曳的曼妙身姿,成为中国人眼中优雅的代表。

④ Furthermore, the flexibility and strength of the bamboo stalk also comes to represent the human values of cultivation and integrity in which one yields but does not break.
此外,竹子的柔韧和力量也用来象征人们高雅的品德和坚忍不拔的正直精神。

---

① "宁可食无肉,不可居无竹"出自苏轼《于潜僧绿筠轩》。
② "采菊东篱下,悠然见南山"出自晋朝陶渊明(约352—427)《饮酒》诗。

⑤ When nearly all the flowers are withered and bare in late autumn, only the chrysanthemums withstand the heavy frost and bloom energetically in graceful shapes and bright colors.
深秋，几乎所有花儿都凋谢枯萎，只有菊花不畏严霜，身姿高雅、色彩明艳地竞相绽放。

Exercises

Task 1 Listening and Speaking

Directions: *Listen to the dialogue twice and answer the following questions.*

(1) How is filial piety based on a hierarchical relationship?

(2) In modern society, what are the responsibilities of parents or elders in the family? Can you give some examples?

(3) What are the responsibilities of children in the family?

(4) Why are Chinese young people urged to get married and have babies?

(5) Why do Chinese people think family is very important?

Task 2 Listening and Summarizing

Directions: *Listen to the Introduction to Four Gentlemen in Plants and summarize the characteristics or human values each plant represents.*

Plants	Characteristics
Plum	(1)_____ and (2)_____ under adverse conditions
Orchid	(3)_____
Bamboo	a metaphor of (4)_____ and (5)_____ relates to a man with (6)_____ and (7)_____ (8)_____ and (9)_____ (10)_____ and (11)_____
Chrysanthemum	to show the (12)_____ of reclusive life

Task 3 Vocabulary Building

Directions: *Complete the following sentences with the words listed below. Change the forms if necessary.*

subtle	desolation	delicate	yield	urge
withstand	striking	tolerance	label	dwell

(1) The _____ of diversity of Chinese culture is represented on its full respect for differences of various nations and cultures.

(2) Women were treated like _____ flowers needing special treatment.

(3) Chinese painting is a pure art which has incomparable refinements (精致) of

design and reveals _____ insights into nature and human beings.

(4) Her death left him with a terrible sense of _____.

(5) Throughout the history of humanity the _____ for artistic expression has been almost as strong as that for food and shelter.

(6) A real gentleman should have the virtue to _____ the temptation.

(7) People were forced to _____ their land to the occupying forces.

(8) Many ancient Chinese literati chose to _____ in hills for reclusive life.

(9) Traditional Chinese women were _____ as reserved, shy, obedient and subordinate to men.

(10) There's a _____ contrast between his deeds and his words.

Translation Practice

Directions: *Translate the following passages into English.*

（1）重视教育和尊敬师长是中国悠久的传统美德。中国的第一部教育学专著《学记》(*The Record of Learning*)提出了"教学为先"的思想。三千年前的周代，国家设立了不同规模不同层次的学校，由官员兼任教师。春秋时期，孔子开办了私学，并提出人无论贵贱都有受教育的权利。对教育的重视决定了教师的地位。中国有许多尊师的说法，如"一日为师，终生为父"。现在，中国还把每年的9月10日定为"教师节"。

（2）孝顺是中国文化中一个重要的美德，指的是一个人对父母和祖先的尊重。历史上儒家经典作品《孝经》(*The Classic of Filial Piety*)。一直被认为是该美德的权威（authoritative）来源。该书介绍了如何利用孝顺建立良好的社会。一般而言，孝顺是指善待和照顾父母，尊敬父母、支持父母、对父母讲礼貌。也指不仅在家对父母在外对他人都要从善，从而为父母带来好名声。虽然中国人一直拥有众多不同宗教信仰，孝顺却几乎是所有人共同的。

Words and Expressions Related to Chinese Traditional Virtues
中国传统美德相关英语词汇和表达方式

Chinese traditional virtues	中国传统美德
Five Constant Virtues	五常
filial piety and fraternal duty	孝悌
sacrificial rites	祭礼
behavioral norms	行为规范
monarch and subjects	君与臣

Unit 9

Virtues

feudal society	封建社会
three obediences and four virtues	三从四德
cultural envoy	文化使者
extended family	大家庭
nuclear family	小家庭
share the same dwelling	居住在同一屋檐下
four gentlemen in plants	植物四君子
nobility of character	品德高尚
moral integrity	道德高尚

Key to Unit 9 Exercises

Before you start

1. Traditional virtues are essence of morality and civilization of Chinese society, most of which originated from Confucianism. They influenced Chinese greatly to form correct values and healthy cultural psychology, and to behave appropriately in the society and family. Even today, they are still the cultural resources as well as the foundation in the moral construction of modern Chinese citizens.

We can easily name a lot of Chinese traditional virtues, like filial piety, i.e. to respect parents and other seniors in the family, benevolence, i.e. to show love for humanity, to help people around, to show justice and sincerity etc.

2. In my opinion, traditional Chinese women were always shy, tender and reserved. And most importantly, they were inferior to men in society and the family. For example, they needed to show obedience to male family members. Most women did not have the right to receive education.

But there were some famous women in ancient China, such as Wu Zetian, the only female emperor in Chinese history; Xi Shi, one of the most beautiful women in China, etc.

Section A Reading and Writing

Task 1 Skimming and Scanning
(1) Y (2) NG (3) Y (4) N (5) N (6) Y (7) Y
(8) truth from falsehood
(9) books and life
(10) deeds, words and mind

Task 2　Discussing and Writing

Sample Writing

With the development of our society, people's traditional values have changed a lot. Many people are inclined to seek after high-quality life, high economic profits and realization of self-value. Under the influence of these changes, some people come to the conclusion that traditional virtues, like thrift, honesty and being happy to help others, are out of date, to which I can't give my consent.

Though some of traditional virtues are meeting greater challenges than before, most people, as the mainstream of our society, still go after these time-honored traditional virtues in their lives. In their eyes, high quality does not mean we can afford to waste. Whether in the past, at present or in the future, thrift is everyone's responsibility. In addition, without honesty, our society and economy will fall into disorder. And without mutual help, human society will stop developing soon.

Considering what has been mentioned above, I think, traditional virtues remain as indispensable elements in the Chinese characters in modern society. Therefore, we must strengthen education on traditional virtues. Only if the whole nation is aware of their eternal value will our traditional virtues take root firmly in our nation's spirits. (192 words)

Task 3　Reading and Blank-Filling

(1) following the rules

(2) morality, proper speech, modest manner and diligent work

(3) created new virtues and images

(4) no differently than/as same as

(5) having scholars write biographies of famous women

(6) had moved three times

(7) his mother's influence and training

(8) the peace and culture envoy

(9) spread the Buddhism

(10) varied cultural and commercial exchanges

Task 4　Translating

(1) The woman with no talent is the one who has merit.

(2) A woman tries to look good for the one who loves her.

(3) Follow the man you have married, be he a fowl or a dog.

(4) Three women will make it a real drama.

(5) helpful wife and wise mother

Unit 9
Virtues

Section B Listening and Speaking

Task 1 **Listening and Speaking**

(1) In the family, the elders have the responsibility to care for the young and raise them properly; while the young in turn have the responsibility to respect and obey the elders.

(2) Parents and elders have the responsibility to provide for children and raise them to have the appropriate qualities. For example, parents teach them how to be a good person; give them every opportunity they possibly can, such as enrolling them in good schools, helping them to get a job and so on.

(3) Children and younger family members are expected to be obedient and to make most of the opportunities elders give them to become successful. And they are also expected to produce children to continue the family line.

(4) Because to follow filial piety younger family members are expected to produce children to continue the family line. And parents always hope their children would have a happy and stable life.

(5) Because people are born into a family or a group and cannot prosper alone, and the success of an individual depends on the harmony and strength of the group; family is the core group of the whole society.

Task 2 **Listening and Summarizing**

(1) inner beauty   (2) strength   (3) elegance   (4) vitality

(5) longevity   (6) exemplary conduct (7) nobility of character

(8) tolerance   (9) open-mindedness   (10) cultivation

(11) integrity   (12) leisure

Task 3 **Vocabulary Building**

(1) tolerance   (2) delicate   (3) subtle   (4) desolation   (5) urge

(6) withstand   (7) yield   (8) dwell   (9) labeled   (10) striking

参考译文

(1) It is a long-standing traditional virtue to value education and respect teachers in China. The first monograph (专著) about education in China, *The Record of Learning*, brought up the idea of "education is the top priority". Three thousand years ago, in the Zhou Dynasty, the government set up schools of different scales and levels with officers as teachers. In the Spring and Autumn Period (春秋时期), Confucius even ran private schools with a slogan (口号) that everyone, rich or poor, had the right to receive education. Respect for education determines the status of teachers. There are a lot of Chinese sayings that show respect towards teachers, such as "A teacher for a day is a father for a lifetime". Nowadays, September the tenth is designated (指定) to be the Teachers' Day in China.

(2) Filial piety is considered a key virtue in Chinese culture, which is about the respect for one's parents and ancestors. The Confucian classic (经典作品), *The Classic of Filial Piety*, has historically been the authoritative source on this virtue. The book is about how to set up a good society based on filial piety. In more general terms, filial piety means to be good to and to take care of one's parents, to show respect, support and courtesy (礼貌) to one's parents. It also means to engage in good conduct (行为) not just towards parents but also towards others outside the home so as to bring a good reputation to one's parents. Although the Chinese have had a diversity of religious beliefs, filial piety has been common to almost all of them.

Unit 10

National Treasures

> **导 读**
>
> 本单元旨在通过对敦煌莫高窟、唐三彩、川剧变脸、清明上河图等中华民族文化瑰宝的介绍,使学生了解相关文化知识和英语表达,并在跨文化交际中更好地承担传播中华文化的使命。

Before You Start

While you are preparing for this unit, consider what you know about the following questions:

1. What do you know about the World Heritage Convention? How many sites in China are on the list of UNESCO World Heritage?
2. What is the most popular local opera in your hometown? What are the features of this opera?

Section A Reading and Writing

Text 1 Dunhuang Mogao Grottoes

① Dunhuang Mogao Grottoes or Dunhuang Mogao Caves, also known as the One-Thousand-Buddha Grottoes(千佛洞), are located on the eastern, rocky side of Mingsha Mountain, near Dunhuang City, Gansu Province. The grottoes are the world's largest and oldest treasure house of Buddhist art. In December 1987, Dunhuang appeared, together with Mount Tai, the Great Wall, the Forbidden City and the Terracotta Warriors(兵马俑), on UNESCO's① World Cultural Heritage List.

---

① UNESCO:联合国教科文组织,全称是 The United Nations Educational, Scientific and Cultural Organization。

Construction of the Mogao Grottoes began in 366 and reached a peak in the Tang Dynasty (618—907), but it was not finished until the Yuan Dynasty (1279—1368). Now there are 492 grottoes in existence, with some 45,000 square meters of murals (壁画) drawn over a period that encompassed (包括) ten dynasties from the Frontal Qin Dynasty①(351—394) to the Yuan Dynasty. It also features 245 painted clay sculptures and five wooden architectural structures of the Tang (618—907) and the Song (907—1279) Dynasties. If we put all the murals of Dunhuang Grottoes together, they would form a 25-kilometer painting corridor, which is unique in the world.

The Mogao Caves have been recognized by UNESCO as a World Heritage Site

The Mogao Grottoes show examples of various types of art, such as architecture, painting and statuary (雕像). ②By inheriting the artistic traditions of the central and western regions of China and absorbing the merits of ancient arts from India, Greece and Iran, ancient Chinese artists created Buddhist art works with strong local features. These art works are treasures of human civilization, providing valuable material for studies of politics, economy, culture, religion, ethnic relations and foreign exchanges of China in old times. Besides, there are also about 50,000 items of printings, wearings, scriptures (经文) and documents written in several languages spanning the period from the Three Kingdoms Period to the Northern Song Dynasty.

Painted clay sculptures and murals in the Mogao Grottoes have mainly Buddhist themes, but they also include human figures, reflecting various societies and cultures of different times. Besides, they also demonstrate painting styles of different times in layout, figure design, delineation(描绘) and coloring as well as the integration of Chinese and Western arts.

Painted clay figures are the main treasures of Dunhuang Grottoes. ③The figures are in different forms, including round figures and relief figures. The tallest is 34.5 meters high, while the smallest is only 2 centimeters. These painted clay figures show such a great variety of themes and subject matters, as well as advanced techniques, that the Mogao Grottoes are generally regarded as the world's leading museum of Buddhist painted clay figures.

---

① the Frontal Qin Dynasty：(十六国时期)的前秦王朝。据传前秦苻坚建元二年(公元366年)有沙门乐尊者行至此处，见鸣沙山上金光万道，状有千佛，于是萌发开凿之心，后历建不断，遂成佛门圣地，号为敦煌莫高窟，俗称千佛洞。

The murals in the Mogao Grottoes display Buddhist sutras(佛经), natural scenery, buildings, flower patterns, and ancient farming and production scenes. There are 1,045 murals extant(现存的), with a total area of 45,000 square meters. They are artistic records of historical changes and customs and traditions from the 4th to the 14th centuries.

The Dunhuang Murals contain rich designs of Buddhas, deities, ghosts, animals, mountains, rivers, architecture and a few decorative patterns. It is a splendid treasure of Buddhist art. The murals present the painting styles and features of different dynasties. In the Dunhuang Murals, we can directly see the development of mural art over ten dynasties and get rich information about many aspects of Chinese culture and history. (561 words)

(Based on http://www.enread.com/entertainment/travel/82,734.htm)

Words and Expressions for Dunhuang Mogao Grottoes
敦煌莫高窟相关英语词汇和表达方式

the world's largest and oldest treasure house of Buddhist art	世界最大最古老的佛教艺术宝藏
reached a peak in the Tang Dynasty	在唐代达到鼎盛
there are 492 grottoes in existence	现存492个窟
painted clay sculptures	彩绘泥塑
spanning the period from the Three Kingdoms Period to the Northern Song Dynasty	横跨三国到北宋数个朝代
the integration of Chinese and Western arts	中西方艺术的融合
1,045 murals extant	现存的1,045幅壁画

Difficult Sentences

① Dunhuang Mogao Grottoes or Dunhuang Mogao Caves, also known as the One-Thousand-Buddha Grottoes, are located on the eastern, rocky side of Mingsha Mountain, near Dunhuang City, Gansu Province.
敦煌莫高窟,俗称千佛洞,位于甘肃省敦煌市附近的鸣沙山东麓断崖上。

② By inheriting the artistic traditions of the central and western regions of China and absorbing the merits of ancient arts from India, Greece and Iran, ancient Chinese artists created Buddhist art works with strong local features.
中国古代的艺术家们通过继承中国中西部地区的艺术传统,并吸收了来自印度、希腊和伊朗的古代艺术魅力,创造出极具地域特色的佛教艺术作品。

③ The figures are in different forms, including round figures and relief figures.

塑像形式各异,包括圆雕①和浮雕②塑像。

Text 2 Tang Tri-Colored Glazed Pottery

河南洛阳唐代墓中发掘出的三彩③动物俑(2012年6月4日摄)。新华社发(张晓理摄)

A type of glazed pottery with the dominant colors of yellow, brown and green was very popular in the Tang Dynasty (618—907). It was later called the tri-colored glazed pottery(陶釉)of the Tang Dynasty, or Tangsancai.

①Tang tri-colored glazed pottery is a low-melting glazed pottery. It is made by adding metallic oxides(金属氧化物) to the colored glaze and calcining(煅烧) the object to create different colors, namely the predominant yellow, brown and green. ②The chemicals in the glaze change gradually in the firing process, creating a variegated(杂色的,斑驳的) effect with a majestic and elegant artistic attraction. Tri-colored glazed pottery is not as practical as the blue and white porcelain(瓷器) that had already emerged at the time.

Tri-colored glazed pottery utensils(器皿) of the Tang are usually rounded and full in shape in accordance with the aesthetic values of the time. ③The accurately proportioned human and animal figures have fluid lines, natural expressions and life-like movements. The soldier figures have strong muscles, big staring eyes and wield(挥) swords or arrows. The female figures have high hair buns(发髻) and full sleeves; they stand gracefully erect, looking natural and elegant. The animal figures are mainly of horses and camels.

A tri-colored glazed pottery of a camel and a dance group was unearthed in a Tang general's tomb. The camel is brown and stands with its head raised high. The long hairs on its head, chest, stomach and upper parts of its two front legs are rendered carefully and

---

① 圆雕作品又称立体雕,是指非压缩的,可以多方位、多角度欣赏的三维立体雕塑。
② 浮雕是雕塑与绘画结合的产物,用压缩的办法来处理对象,靠透视等因素来表现三维空间,并只供一面或两面观看。
③ 三彩釉陶始于南北朝而盛于唐朝,它以造型生动逼真、色泽艳丽和富有生活气息而著称,因为常用黄、褐、绿三种基本色,又在唐代形成特点,所以被后人称为"唐三彩"。古人多用于殉葬。

beautifully. On the camel's back is a platform covered by a rug with two ethnic musicians sitting with their backs to each other, playing instruments. A third ethnic person dances beside them. The three human figures have deep eyes, high-bridged noses and full beards; they are wearing long, green sweaters with turned-down collars and white boots. The one in the front has a deep yellow coat. This piece of pottery is truly an exquisite handicraft.

Tri-colored glazed pottery of the Tang Dynasty was mostly produced in Xi'an, Luoyang and Yangzhou, which were important cities along the Silk Road. The camel was the major form of transportation tool on the ancient trade route during the Tang Dynasty. From the glazed pottery, we can imagine the travelers and camels making their hard journey across the desert, depending on each other for survival. The large figures and resolute expressions of the camels represent the hardships of traveling on the long and ancient Silk Road.

④Tri-colored glazed pottery is the cream of the Tang Dynasty pottery and it flourished during the dynasty's early and middle period. As the Tang Dynasty gradually lost its power and the technology of producing porcelain quickly developed, tri-colored glazed pottery production declined. Though tri-colored glazed pottery was also produced in the Liao and the Jin Dynasties, it was not made in such great numbers and its quality was not as good as that of the Tang Dynasty.

Tri-colored glazed pottery was exported to foreign countries in the early Tang Dynasty and won great favor. It has always been famed for its bright colors and pleasing shapes. It is a shining pearl among ancient Chinese pottery. (527 words)

(Based on http://english.ccnt.com.cn/?catog＝fineart&file＝40,300&page＝2&ads＝service_001)

Words and Expressions for Tang Tri-colored Glazed Pottery
唐三彩相关英语词汇和表达方式

Tri-colored Glazed Pottery	三彩釉陶
in accordance with the aesthetic values of the time	与当时的审美价值观一致
high hair buns	梳得很高的发髻
full sleeves	宽大的衣袖
an exquisite handicraft	精美的手工艺品
won great favor	赢得盛誉

Difficult Sentences

① Tang tri-colored glazed pottery is a low-melting glazed pottery. It was made by adding metallic oxides to the colored glaze and calcining (煅烧) the object to create different colors, namely the predominant yellow, brown and green.

唐三彩是一种低温釉陶器，在色釉中加入不同的金属氧化物，经过煅烧便形成多种色彩，但多以黄、褐、绿三色为主。

② The chemicals in the glaze change gradually in the firing process, creating a variegated effect with a majestic and elegant artistic attraction.

色釉中的化学物质在煅烧过程中逐渐发生变化，最后形成色彩斑斓的效果，具有高贵典雅的艺术魅力。

③ The accurately proportioned human and animal figures have fluid lines, natural expressions and life-like movements.

比例匀称的人物和动物造型线条流畅，表情自然，栩栩如生。

④ Tri-colored glazed pottery is the cream of the Tang Dynasty pottery and it flourished during the dynasty's early and middle period.

唐三彩是唐代陶器中的精华，在初唐、盛唐时达到巅峰。

Exercises

Task 1　Reading Comprehension

Directions: *Read Text 1 and answer the following questions by selecting one correct answer from A, B, C, or D for each question.*

(1) Which of the following was not inscribed in 1987 on the list of UNESCO World Heritage?

　　A. The Great Wall.

　　B. The Terracotta Warriors.

　　C. The Ancient City of Ping Yao.

　　D. Dunhuang Mogao Grottoes.

(2) Construction of the Mogao Grottoes began in _____ and was finished in _____.

　　A. 366; the Tang Dynasty

　　B. the Frontal Qin Dynasty; the Song Dynasty

　　C. the 4th century; the Song Dynasty

　　D. the Frontal Qin Dynasty; the 14th century

(3) Which of the following is not mentioned as a type of art shown in the Mogao Grottoes?

　　A. Porcelain　　B. Statuary　　C. Architecture　　D. Painting

(4) Besides the murals, there are about 50,000 items including scriptures and documents, etc. which covered the period from _____ to _____.

　　A. the Tang Dynasty; the Yuan Dynasty

　　B. the Three Kingdoms Period; the Northern Song Dynasty

Unit 10 National Treasures

    C. the Frontal Qin Dynasty; the Song Dynasty

    D. the Three Kingdoms Period; the Yuan Dynasty

(5) Why are the Mogao Grottoes viewed as the world's best museum of Buddhist painted clay figures?

    A. Because the figures in the Mogao Grottoes are in various forms.

    B. Because the figures in the Mogao Grottoes reflect different societies.

    C. Because the figures in the Mogao Grottoes demonstrate the integration of Chinese and Western arts.

    D. Because the figures in the Mogao Grottoes show various Buddhist themes and advanced techniques.

Task 2 Researching and Writing

Directions: *Besides the Mogao Grottoes, what are the other famous grottoes in China? Choose one and carry a research on it. Then write an essay of no less than 150 words about it.*

Task 3 Thinking and Judging

Directions: *Read Text 2 and judge whether the following statements are true (T), false (F) or not given (NG).*

True   if the statement agrees with the information mentioned in the passage

False   if the statement contradicts the information mentioned in the passage

Not Given   if there is no information on this in the passage

(1) The predominant colors of Tang tri-colored glazed pottery are yellow, brown and green. (　)

(2) Compared with the blue and white porcelain, Tang tri-colored glazed pottery bears more artistic attraction other than practical values. (　)

(3) The shape or style of the utensils of Tang tri-colored glazed pottery created a sharp contrast to the aesthetic values of the time. (　)

(4) In the Tang Dynasty, every city along the Silk Road produced tri-colored glazed pottery. (　)

(5) Tang tri-colored glazed pottery was at its peak in the Tang Dynasty and then went downhill with the decline of the Empire. (　)

Task 4 Research and Development

Directions: *Make a further study on Tang tri-colored glazed pottery and give a presentation to the class analyzing how Tang tri-colored glazed pottery reflected prosperity of the Tang Dynasty.*

Section B Listening and Speaking

Text 3 Situational Dialogue: Face-Changing in Sichuan Opera

Peter: Hey, I watched a performance called face-changing yesterday. It's amazing!

Yang: Face-changing? Oh! It's a famous art form in my hometown.

Peter: Really? I was told that face-changing is closely related to Sichuan Opera?

Yang: Right. We cannot talk about face-changing without mentioning Sichuan Opera. Sichuan Opera is one of the many local operas in China, popular in the provinces of Sichuan, Yunnan and Guizhou.

Peter: I think the actors are like magicians. ①They change their facial masks in quick succession and every mask shows different emotional feelings of the character in the opera.

Yang: You're right. But we call the facial mask *lian pu*, which is the facial make-up typical of Chinese opera. The changing of the types and colors of *lian pu* reflects a character's mood. For instance, red represents anger and black represents extreme fury.

Peter: It's interesting. Tell me more about it.

Yang: Ok. Face-changing began 300 years ago, during the reign of Emperor Qianlong in the Qing Dynasty, who lived in the 18th century.

Peter: Oh, that's too old.

Yang: Yeah, it has a long history. Face-changing was first used in a story about a hero who stole from the rich to help the poor. When he was caught by feudal officials, he changed his face to puzzle them and escaped as a result.

Peter: Wow, he was so cool. But how did the actors do this in the opera?

Yang: Opera masters changed the color of their faces by blowing into a bowl of red, black or gold powder at the beginning. The powder would adhere to their oiled skin quickly. Another method is to hide the colored paste in the performers' palms. Actors would then mop it up onto their faces.

Peter: Smart people! I should say.

Yang: Very smart! But by the 1920s, opera masters began using layers of masks made of oiled paper or dried pig bladder (膀胱).

Peter: Pig bladder! How could they think of that? Do actors still use it nowadays?

Yang: No, they don't. ②Modern-day masters use full-face painted silk masks, which can be worn in layers of as many as twenty-four, and be pulled off one by one.

Peter: And they must do it very quickly?

Yang: Yeah. Skilled performers could peel off one mask after another in less than a second.

Peter: Less than a second! It's unbelievable! ③ It seems that face-changing is not simply changing one's facial makeup in a casual way; it needs special techniques.

Yang: Exactly. ④ Face-changing techniques generally fall into three categories, "wiping face", "blowing face" and "pulling face".

Peter: What do they mean? You need to explain.

Yang: Ok. "Wiping" means that the paint is put on a certain part of the face in advance, and the actor spreads the paint over the face while performing, then the "face" is changed.

Peter: I see. And what about "blowing"? Blowing powder or something?

Yang: You bet. "Blowing" is only employed when powder cosmetics are used. On the stage, a tiny box with powder cosmetics in it is placed beforehand. ⑤ A movement of prostration (俯卧) near the box will enable the performer to blow the powder onto his face.

Peter: And then the color of his face is changed. But the actor must be skillful. Otherwise, the powder will be blown into his eyes or mouth.

Yang: Right. The actor has to close his eyes.

Peter: So in this sense, "blowing" is relatively more complicated.

Yang: Yeah. But "pulling" is the most troublesome among the three skills. ⑥ When one is going to use the "pulling" technique, he has to draw facial masks on fine pieces of silk cloth, cut them into the right size, tie a thin thread to each mask and stick them onto his face before the performance. The threads are fastened to somewhere hidden in his costumes. Many performers prefer to tie them onto their waistbands. When performing, the actor would pull the masks off one after another under the cover of various dancing movements.

Peter: You're right. It is the most troublesome. On the one hand, the dancing movements have to be natural, but on the other, the action of pulling should be invisible to the audience. If the audience sees through the trick, they would probably get dissatisfied and pull a face too! (733 words)

(Based on http://www.hjenglish.com/page/195,892/)

Words and Expressions for Face-Changing in Sichuan Opera
川剧变脸相关英语词汇和表达方式

during the reign of Emperor Qianlong in the Qing Dynasty	在清朝乾隆统治时期
feudal official	封建官吏
adhere to	黏附在……上；坚持；遵循
to hide the colored paste in the performers' palms	把颜料藏在表演者的手掌里
layers of masks	一层层的面具

Difficult Sentences

① They change their facial masks in quick succession and every mask shows different emotional feelings of the character in the opera.

他们以飞快的速度一张一张地更换脸谱，每张脸谱都表现了戏剧人物不同的情感。

② Modern-day masters use full-face painted silk masks, which can be worn in layers of as many as twenty-four, and be pulled off one by one.

如今的演员们用的是画在丝绸上的脸谱，这种脸谱能在脸上贴 24 张，表演时再一张一张地把它们扯下来。

③ It seems that face-changing is not simply changing one's facial makeup in a casual way; it needs special techniques.

变脸可不是随便化化妆，改变一下自己的脸谱。它需要特殊技法。

④ Face-changing techniques generally fall into three categories, "wiping face", "blowing face" and "pulling face".

变脸技法大体上可以分为三种："抹脸"、"吹脸"和"扯脸"。

⑤ A movement of prostration near the box will enable the performer to blow the powder onto his face.

演员（表演时）在盒子附近做一个伏地的舞蹈动作，趁机将粉末吹在脸上。

⑥ When one is going to use the "pulling" technique, he has to draw facial masks on fine pieces of silk cloth, cut them into the right size, tie a thin thread to each mask and stick them onto his face before the performance. The threads are fastened to somewhere hidden in his costumes. Many performers prefer to tie them onto their waistbands. When performing, the actor would pull the mask off one after another under the cover of various dancing movements.

"扯脸"是事先将脸谱画在一张一张的绸子上，剪好，每张脸谱上都系一根丝线，再一张一张地贴在脸上。丝线则系在衣服的某个地方，但不能让别人看出来，很多人常常把它系在腰带上。表演时，在各种舞蹈动作的掩护下，再一张一张地将它们扯下来。

Unit 10

National Treasures

Text 4 *The Qingming Festival by the Riverside*

Many ancient Chinese paintings contain the seals and signatures of both the painters and the collectors. There is one famous Chinese painting, *The Qingming Festival by the Riverside*, which is covered with innumerable signatures and seals, indicating it had been in the hands of many private and official collectors. The painting survived many calamities and historical shifts and was handed down to the present; some collectors even sacrificed their lives in order to preserve this art treasure.

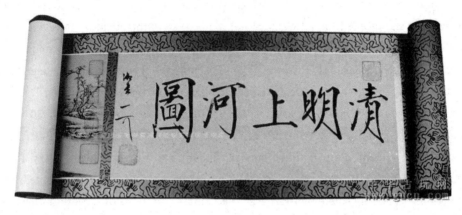

The picture was done by the painter Zhang Zeduan[①] in the Northern Song Dynasty (960—1127). He was a native of Shandong Province and studied painting in his early years in Bianjing（汴京,今河南开封）, the capital of the Northern Song Dynasty. Later he became a painter of the Imperial Painting Academy of the Northern Song Dynasty. Though there are not many historical records of him, his name is remembered simply due to this masterpiece.

The Qingming Festival by the Riverside is a long colored painted scroll（画卷）with a length of 528cm and a height of 24.8cm. It portrays the noisy street scenes of Bianjing during the Qingming Festival (a festival for the mourning of ancestors). During that time, people kept the custom of going to street fairs on the festival. The painting features magnificent and complex scenes with a rigorous structure, which can be divided into three parts: scenes of the suburbs, the Bian River and the city streets.

In the suburban scenes, farmers are working in the fields and wealthy people are returning from mourning their ancestors. The street is crowded with people on horseback,

---

① 张择端(1085—1145),东武(今山东诸城)人。宣和年间任翰林待诏,专事绘画,为北宋末年杰出的现实主义画家。存世作品长卷风俗画《清明上河图》创作于宋徽宗宣和年间(1119—1125)。该画的主题是描写北宋都城汴京(今河南开封)社会各阶层之生活情景,是中国十大传世名画之一。全图规模宏大,笔法细致古雅,卷后有金代张著、张公药、元代杨准,明代吴宽、李东阳、冯保等13家题跋。此画的第一位收藏人是宋徽宗,他用瘦金体亲笔在画上题写了"清明河图"五个字。明清两朝,此画均归皇室收藏。1925年溥仪将该画携出故宫,后流落到东北长春一带,现藏故宫博物院,属国宝级文物。

wheel carts and sedan chairs. The scenes of the Bian River are the most magnificent part of the painting. The arch bridge stands like a rainbow over the river; on the bridge are streams of people bustling about, and under the bridge are numerous boats competing to move forward. Some interesting scenes are drawn in great detail. ①For instance, a horse has shied（惊退）on the bridge, scaring a donkey and attracting many onlookers.

Bianjing was the political, economic and cultural center of the Northern Song Dynasty. Its important role in the empire is fully depicted in the scenes of the city streets. The streets are lined with government mansions, residential courtyards, workshops, teahouses and grocery shops. ②Various wagons and people from all walks of life can be seen in the picture, conveying an exciting and bustling atmosphere. ③The scenes in the picture are carefully arranged, forming interesting contrasts and a good sense of rhythm. The depiction of the architecture, merchants and transportation in Bianjing vividly reflects the economic boom of the Northern Song Dynasty.

There are over 550 human figures, some 60 animals, 20 wooden boats, 30 rooms and pavilions（凉亭）, and about 20 vehicles of various kinds in *The Qingming Festival by the Riverside*. Few ancient pictures have such rich content. Furthermore, every figure and every detailed scene are arranged strategically, creating chaos（混乱）that appears to have some order to it. All these elements reveal the painter's careful observation of life and his supreme painting skills.

The Qingming Festival by the Riverside is a great and rare realistic painting. At the same time, it provides vivid visual depiction about business, handicrafts, architecture and transportation in the metropolis of the Northern Song Dynasty. (547 words)

(Based on http://www.chinaculture.org/gb/en_artqa/2003-09/24/content_39764.htm)

Words and Expressions for *The Qingming Festival by the Riverside*
《清明上河图》相关英语词汇和表达方式

the seals and signatures	印章和签名
The painting survived many calamities and historical shifts.	画卷历经重重灾难和无数历史变迁最终得以保存下来。
a long colored painted scroll with a length of 528cm and a height of 24.8cm	一幅长528厘米，高24.8厘米的彩色画卷
Imperial Painting Academy of the Northern Song Dynasty	北宋皇家翰林画院
street fairs	街上的集市
rigorous structure	结构严谨

Unit 10

National Treasures

bustle about	忙碌；东奔西跑
fully depicted in the scenes of the city streets	在画里的城市街景中得以充分体现
creating chaos that appears to have some order to it	制造的混乱景象中似乎又蕴含着某种秩序
the painter's careful observation of life	画家对生活的细致入微的观察
supreme painting skills	高超的绘画技艺

Difficult Sentences

① For instance, a horse has shied on the bridge, scaring a donkey and attracting many onlookers.
例如，桥上一匹受惊的马又吓坏了一头驴，从而引来众多围观者。

② Various wagons and people from all walks of life can be seen in the picture, conveying an exciting and bustling atmosphere.
各种马车和各行各业的人们都在画面上描绘出来，展现出热闹喧嚣的氛围。

③ The scenes in the picture are carefully arranged, forming interesting contrasts and a good sense of rhythm.
画面的景物经过精心安排，错落有致，形成鲜明有趣的对比。

Exercises

Task 1　Listening and Focusing

Directions: *Listen to the situational dialogue and focus on the different methods employed in face-changing. Then try to fill in the blanks.*

At the beginning opera masters changed the color of their face by ___(1)___ a bowl of red, black or gold powder. The powder would ___(2)___ quickly. Another method is to ___(3)___ in the performers' ___(4)___. Actors would then ___(5)___ onto their faces with oil. And by the 1920s, opera masters began using ___(6)___ made of oiled paper or dried pig bladder. But nowadays masters use full-face ___(7)___, which can be ___(8)___ of as many as twenty-four, and be pulled off one by one. Skilled performers could ___(9)___ one mask after another in ___(10)___.

Task 2　Listening and Matching

Directions: *Listen to the dialogue again, and select the appropriate features from the answer choices and match them to the specific face-changing techniques that they describe.*

Answer Choices	Specific Technique
A. The actor pulls the masks off one after another under the cover of dancing movements. B. Facial masks are drawn on pieces of silk cloth. C. The actor has to close his eyes. D. The paint is put on a certain part of the face beforehand. E. Powder cosmetics are used. F. A movement of prostration is needed. G. Each mask with a thin thread is stuck onto the actor's face. H. The actor spreads the paint over the face while performing. I. It is the most troublesome among the three skills. J. A tiny box with powder cosmetics in it is placed on the stage in advance.	Wiping face Blowing face Pulling face

Task 3 Listening, Imitating and Summarizing

Directions: *Listen to the dialogue twice and try to introduce the face-changing to the class in your own words.*

Task 4 Listening and Detailing

Directions: *Listen to the lecture and complete the following information.*

(1) *The Qingming Festival by the Riverside* is different from other ancient Chinese paintings in that it contained _____, which indicates it had been in the hands of many private and official collectors.

(2) The length of *The Qingming Festival by the Riverside* is _____ and its height is _____.

(3) With a rigorous structure, the scenes of the painting can be divided into three parts: _____, _____ and _____.

(4) Of the three parts of the scenes, _____ are the most magnificent part of the painting.

(5) *The Qingming Festival by the Riverside* vividly depicts _____, _____, _____ and _____ in the metropolis of the Northern Song Dynasty.

Task 5 Listening and Writing

Directions: *Listen to the lecture again and summarize its main points; then write a* short passage introducing a famous ancient Chinese painter.

Translation Practice

Directions: *Translate the following passages into English.*

(1) 敦煌莫高窟(Dunhuang Mogao Grottoes)，也称千佛洞，位于甘肃省敦煌市附近的鸣沙山东麓石崖上。它被认为是世界上最大最古老的佛教艺术宝藏。莫高窟的修建始于366年，在唐代达到鼎盛，但到了元朝才竣工。现存492个窟和1045幅壁画(mural)，以及245座彩绘泥塑(clay sculpture)和5个唐宋时期的木质建筑结构。除此之外，莫高窟还存有大量的横跨三国到北宋数个朝代的经文(scripture)、文献和绘画。敦煌莫高窟展示出各类艺术形式的精华，同时也体现了中西方的艺术融合。

(2)《清明上河图》(*The Qingming Festival by the Riverside*)是由北宋画家张择端(1085—1145)创作完成的。它是一幅长528厘米，宽24.8厘米的彩色画卷。该画描述了清明节北宋都城汴京(今河南开封)热闹的街景。整幅画可以分成三部分：郊区景、汴河景以及城市街景。汴河景是该画最为壮观的一部分；而作为政治、经济、文化中心的汴京在北宋的重要地位则在城市街景中得以充分体现。画卷对汴京的建筑、商人和交通的描绘形象地勾勒出北宋的经济繁荣景象。《清明上河图》是一幅伟大的稀世罕见的现实主义画卷。

Key to Unit 10 Exercises

Before You Start

1. What do you know about the World Heritage Convention? How many sites in China are inscribed on the list of UNESCO World Heritage?

    Sample:

    The idea of creating an international movement for protecting heritage emerged after World War I.

    The most significant feature of the 1972 World Heritage Convention is that it links together in a single document the concepts of nature conservation and the preservation of cultural properties. The Convention recognizes the way in which people interact with nature, and the fundamental need to preserve the balance between the two.

    The Convention defines the kind of natural or cultural sites which can be considered for inscription on the World Heritage List. It sets out the duties of State Parties in identifying potential sites and their role in protecting and preserving them. It also explains how the World Heritage Fund is to be used and managed and under what conditions international financial assistance may be provided.

    By the end of 2012, there are 43 World Heritage sites in China, of which 30 are cultural heritage sites, 9 natural sites and 4 cultural and natural sites. The success of an application for the World Heritage site will not only raise the profile of the site internationally, it will also stimulate the local economy. Furthermore, the World Heritage sites enjoy financial assistance and technical support provided by UNESCO.

World Heritage Sites in China:

◆ **Cultural Heritage Sites:**

English Name	Chinese Name	Time
Imperial Palaces of the Ming and Qing Dynasties in Beijing and Shenyang	北京故宫、沈阳故宫	1987
Mausoleum of the First Qin Emperor	秦始皇陵	1987
Mogao Caves	敦煌莫高窟	1987
The Great Wall	长城	1987
Peking Man Site at Zhoukoudian	北京周口店北京猿人遗址	1987
Mountain Resort and Its Outlying Temples, Chengde	承德避暑山庄及周围寺庙	1994
Ancient Building Complex in the Wudang Mountains	武当山古建筑群	1994
Historic Ensemble of the Potala Palace, Lhasa	西藏拉萨布达拉宫系列历史景观	1994
Temple and Cemetery of Confucius and the Kong Family Mansion in Qufu	曲阜孔庙、孔林、孔府	1994
Lushan National Park	庐山国家公园	1996
Ancient City of Ping Yao	平遥古城	1997
Old Town of Lijiang	丽江古城	1997
Classical Gardens of Suzhou	苏州古典园林	1997
Summer Palace, an Imperial Garden in Beijing	北京皇家园林颐和园	1998
Temple of Heaven: an Imperial Sacrificial Altar in Beijing	北京天坛	1998
Dazu Rock Carvings	大足石刻	1999
Imperial Tombs of the Ming and Qing Dynasties	明清皇家陵寝	2000
Longmen Grottoes	龙门石窟	2000
Mount Qingcheng and the Dujiangyan Irrigation System	青城山—都江堰	2000
Ancient Villages in Southern Anhui — Xidi and Hongcun	皖南古村落—西递、宏村	2000
Yungang Grottoes	云冈石窟	2001
Capital Cities and Tombs of the Ancient Koguryo Kingdom	高句丽王城、王陵及贵族墓葬（吉林集安）	2004
Historic Centre of Macao	澳门历史城区	2005
Yin Xu	安阳殷墟	2006
Kaiping Diaolou and Villages	开平碉楼与村落（广东）	2007
Fujian *Tulou*	福建土楼（永定、南靖、华安）	2008
Mount Wutai	五台山	2009

续表

English Name	Chinese Name	Time
Historic Monuments of Dengfeng in "The Centre of Heaven and Earth"	登封"天地之中"历史建筑群（郑州）	2010
West Lake Cultural Landscape of Hangzhou	杭州西湖文化景观	2011
Site of Xanadu	元上都遗址	2012

◆ **Natural Heritage Sites：**

English Name	Chinese Name	Time
Wulingyuan Scenic and Historic Interest Area	武陵源风景名胜区（湖南）	1992
Huanglong Scenic and Historic Interest Area	黄龙风景名胜区（四川）	1992
Jiuzhaigou Valley Scenic and Historic Interest Area	九寨沟风景名胜区	1992
Three Parallel Rivers of Yunnan Protected Areas	三江并流（云南）	2003
Sichuan Giant Panda Sanctuaries — Wolong, Mt Siguniang and Jiajin Mountains	四川大熊猫栖息——卧龙、四姑娘山和夹金山脉	2006
South China Karst	中国南方喀斯特（云南、贵州、重庆市）	2007
Mount Sanqingshan National Park	三清山国家公园（江西）	2008
China Danxia	中国丹霞（包括中国西南部亚热带地区的6处景观）	2010
Chengjiang Fossil Site	澄江化石遗址（云南）	2012

◆ **Cultural and Natural Heritage Sites（Mixed Heritage Sites）：**

English Name	Chinese Name	Time
Mount Taishan or Mount Tai	泰山	1987
Mount Huangshan or the Yellow Mountain	黄山	1990
Mount Emei and Leshan Giant Buddha Scenic Area	峨眉山和乐山大佛	1996
Mount Wuyi	武夷山	1999

2. What is the most popular local opera in your hometown? What are the features of this opera?

Sample：

Yue Opera is the most popular local opera in my hometown. It is on the list of five dominant Chinese operas, and it ranks the second place. It has been inscribed into the National Intangible Cultural Heritage List in 2006.

In the early 20th century, a form of opera called Luodi Changshu（落地唱书）was popular in the area of Shengxian County in Shaoxing, Zhejiang Province. It was named "Yue Opera" because it has its origin in the part of Yue State in the Spring and Autumn

Period dating back about 2000 years ago. They were also called "Didu troupes"(的笃班). At that time, the most outstanding Didu troupe in Shaoxing consisted of only male performers. In the late 1920s, with the emergence of a large number of female performers, a Didu troupe with only female performers appeared; it was called the Women's Refined Opera. In the autumn of 1938, it formally adopted the name of Yue Opera.

The women artists replaced the Mu Biao system (幕表制)(Each drama used to have only an outline, rather than a script; actors performed as they wished, but within the outline.) with scripts. The operas now had definite directors.

Absorbing the elements of Shaoxing Opera, Yue Opera created its own type of music. It is excellent at expressing emotions through singing. In the 1950s, a reform of Yue Opera started under the influence of Yuan Xuefen (袁雪芬). Maintaining its soft, sweet tunes and melodies, and gentle and refined style, Yue Opera adopted artistic achievements from the modern drama Kunqu and western music, in an attempt to create a new performing style. A special kind of ancient costume was created, modern stage settings and lights were introduced, and some western musical instruments were incorporated in the orchestra.

Xiao Bai Hua Yue Opera Troupe (小百花越剧团) is a very famous troupe, which produced many well-known plays, such as: *Butterfly Lovers*, *A Dream of Red Mansions*, *The Romance of the West Chamber* (《西厢记》), *The Han Palace in Sorrow* (《汉宫怨》), *Lu You and Tang Wan*, etc.

Section A Reading and Writing

Exercises

Task 1 **Reading Comprehension**
    (1) C   (2) D   (3) A   (4) B   (5) D

Task 2 **Thinking and Writing**
    Sample Writing

Longmen Grottoes, one of the three great grottoes sites in China, are located 12km south to the city of Luoyang, where there is the Yi River. And on the two sides of the river are Fragrant Mountain and Longmen Mountain. During the 400 years from Northern Wei to later Tang dynasty, the workers and artistic designers were sweating on the caves and temples on the two mountains, and hence made the world famous treasury of stone carving art. Longmen Grottoes are 1km long from north to south; there are all together more than 97,000 statues of Buddha, more than 1300 caves, more than 3,600 inscriptions and titled tablets.

Unit 10

National Treasures

Fengxian Temple is the biggest cave in Longmen Grottoes, which is 30-meter in length and width. The wonder of Fengxian Temple lies in its huge Lushena statue in the central place; it is indeed a wonderful artistic work.

Lushena statue is 17.14 meters in height, her head is 4-meter high, and has two 1.9-meter long ears. According to Buddhist Scripture, Lushena means illumination. This statue has heavy features, her curving lips show kindness, her head lowers down a little as if she is in deep thinking; she resembles a middle-aged lady, deserves respect but not fear. The critics say the artistic workers integrated exalted sentiment, rich emotions, wide vision and classic appearance into one perfect unity during their construction; hence the statue contains boundless charm.

Task 3 Thinking and Judging

(1) T (2) T (3) F (4) NG (5) T

Task 4 Research and Development

Sample Writing

China's feudal society had its heyday under the Tang Dynasty (618—907), and it is reflected in the funerary objects of the Tang Dynasty, especially those built when Emperor Gao Zong and Empress Wu Zetian reigned supreme, which mirror the dynasty's economic prosperity and military might. Legendary animal figures supposedly to protect tomb owners were gone, and in their place were fierce-looking guardian gods with animal figures underfoot. Also found in Tang tombs are figurines of civil and military officials in formal attire (服装). Colorful steeds (战马) replaced ox carts in tombs of the long period from the Southern-Northern Dynasties to the Sui Dynasty.

The Tang Dynasty gave birth to tri-color glazed pottery figurines, which are thought to represent the peak of ancient Chinese pottery sculptural art. Under the reign of Emperor Xuan Zong, extravagance and wastefulness characterized the lifestyle. Female figurines produced during this period invariably have chubby faces and are in well filled-out shapes, with high hair buns, long skirts and composed facial expressions, which, on the other hand, indicates the social peace at the time.

The better known tri-color pottery steeds unearthed from a tomb built in the year 723 for General Xianyu Tinghai also mirror the extravagance and economic prosperity. These animals are all more than 50 centimeters tall. Two of them are white, the other two are yellow with white hooves and white stripes round their long necks. The saddles and bridles are colorful with decorative patterns of golden flowers and leaves. Two of the horses have on their manes (鬃毛) a three-flower pattern popular at the time, and the manes of the other two each bear a single pattern.

Another masterpiece unearthed from the same tomb is a camel carrying four musicians and a dancer on its back. The dancer, in green costumes, obviously belongs to an ethnic minority group of China. This masterpiece reflects the national unity and political stability the dynasty was able to enjoy.

Section B Listening and Speaking

Exercises

Task 1 Listening and Focusing

(1) blowing into   (2) adhere to their oiled skin   (3) hide the colored paste

(4) palms   (5) mop it up   (6) layers of masks

(7) painted silk masks   (8) worn in layers

(9) peel off   (10) less than a second

Task 2 Listening and Matching

Answer Choices	Specific Technique
A. The actor pulls the masks off one after another under the cover of dancing movements.	
B. Facial masks are drawn on pieces of silk cloth.	
C. The actor has to close his eyes.	Wiping face
D. The paint is put on a certain part of the face beforehand.	
E. Powder cosmetics are used.	D, H
F. A movement of prostration is needed.	
G. Each mask with a thin thread is stuck onto the actor's face.	Blowing face
H. The actor spreads the paint over the face while performing.	C, E, F, J
I. It is the most troublesome among the three skills.	Pulling face
J. A tiny box with powder cosmetics in it is placed on the stage in advance.	A, B, G, I

Task 3 Listening, Imitating and Summarizing

Sample Writing:

Face-changing is a special technique in the performance of Sichuan Opera. It began 300 years ago. At the beginning opera masters changed the color of their faces by blowing into a bowl of red, black or gold powder. The powder would adhere to their oiled skin quickly.

Another method is: actors would smear their faces with colored paste concealed in the palms of their hands.

The changing of the types and colors of *lian pu* reflects a character's mood: for example, red represents anger and black represents extreme fury.

Face-changing techniques generally fall into three categories, "wiping face", "blowing face" and "pulling face". In practice, "wiping" is most employed because it is the simplest, while "blowing" is relatively more complicated since one has to close his eyes when blowing in case the powder would fly into his eyes. However, "pulling" is the most troublesome among the three skills.

Task 4　Listening and Detailing

(1) innumerable signatures and seals

(2) 528cm; 24.8cm

(3) scenes of the suburbs; the Bian River; the city streets

(4) the scenes of the Bian River

(5) business; handicrafts; architecture; transportation

Task 5　Listening and Writing

Sample Writing

Zheng Xie (郑燮, 1693—1765), commonly known as Zheng Banqiao, was a native of Xinghua, Jiangsu Province. Born into a poor family, Zheng lived with his wet nurse at a very young age. He learned to paint during his childhood from his father, and then made a living selling his paintings. With support from his friends, Zheng got the opportunity to study and took part in the imperial examination and later served as a county magistrate (知县) in Shandong Province. During his 12 years as an official, Zheng gained the respect of many people. However, unwilling to yield to the philistine (市侩的) ways of the official circle, he later resigned. Zheng then lived in Yangzhou selling his paintings to earn a living. He expressed his true feelings in paintings and gained high achievements.

Zheng was good at drawing orchids (兰花), bamboo and stones. He was adept in Xie Yi (freehand) ink and wash (水墨画) and raised the theory of the three steps of painting — having bamboo in one's eyes, hands and heart. Bamboo in Zheng's paintings was the embodiment of his thoughts and character. His technique involved both dry-brush and wet-brush stroke, including forceful strokes. Zheng stressed the combination of poetry, calligraphy and painting, adding lines from poems to his paintings to bring out the themes. This theory became a feature of the scholar painting.

Zheng's calligraphy and paintings were of a high artistic value. He created a style by combining the orchid-line drawing with calligraphy. His strokes sometimes were as graceful as orchid leaves or as forceful as bamboo leaves.

Apart from painting and calligraphy, Zheng was very fond of literature. Many of his works of literature were about the lives of ordinary people, told in a simple and natural style.

(Based on http://www.chinaculture.org/gb/en_artqa/2003-09/24/content_39699.htm)

参考译文

1) Dunhuang Mogao Grottoes, also known as the One-Thousand-Buddha Grottoes, are located on the eastern, rocky side of Mingsha Mountain, near the city of Dunhuang, Gansu Province. They are regarded as the world's largest and oldest treasure house of Buddhist art. Construction of the Mogao Grottoes began in 366 and reached a peak in the Tang Dynasty, but it was not finished until the Yuan Dynasty. Now there are 492 grottoes and 1,045 murals(壁画) in existence. It also features 245 painted clay sculptures(彩绘泥塑) and five wooden architectural structures of the Tang and the Song Dynasties. Besides, there are also a lot of items of scriptures(经文), documents and paintings spanning the period from the Three Kingdoms Period to the Northern Song Dynasty. The Mogao Grottoes show examples of various types of art and demonstrate the integration of Chinese and Western arts.

2) The *Qingming Festival by the Riverside* (or *Along the River during the Qingming Festival*) is a painting attributed to the artist Zhang Zeduan (1085—1145) in the Song Dynasty. It is a long colored painted scroll with a length of 528cm and a height of 24.8cm. It portrays the busy street scenes of the capital city Bianjing (now Kaifeng, Henan Province) during the Qingming Festival. The painting can be divided into three parts: scenes of the suburbs, the Bian River, and the city streets. The scenes of the Bian River are the most magnificent part of the painting. As Bianjing is the political, economic and cultural center of the Northern Song Dynasty, its importance in the empire is fully depicted in the scenes of the city streets. The depiction of the architecture, merchants and transportation in Bianjing vividly reflects the economic boom of the Northern Song Dynasty. *The Qingming Festival by the Riverside* is a great and rare realistic painting.